The ArtScroll Series®

Rabbi Nosson Scherman / Rabbi Meir Zlotowitz
General Editors

BAR MITZVAH

ITS OBSERVANCE AND SIGNIFICANCE

By:
Rabbi Yaakov Salomon
Rabbi Yonah Weinrib

Overview by:
Rabbi Nosson Scherman

Illumination and Calligraphy by
Rabbi Yonah Weinrib

בר מצוה

A compendium of laws, rituals, and customs anthologized
from Talmudic, Midrashic, and traditional sources

Published by

Mesorah Publications, ltd.

FIRST EDITION
First Impression . . . September, 1991

Published and Distributed by
MESORAH PUBLICATIONS, Ltd.
Brooklyn, New York 11232

Distributed in Israel by
MESORAH MAFITZIM / J. GROSSMAN
Rechov Harav Uziel 117
Jerusalem, Israel

Distributed in Europe by
J. LEHMANN HEBREW BOOKSELLERS
20 Cambridge Terrace
Gateshead, Tyne and Wear
England NE8 1RP

Distributed in Australia & New Zealand by
GOLD'S BOOK & GIFT CO.
36 William Street
Balaclava 3183, Vic., Australia

Distributed in South Africa by
KOLLEL BOOKSHOP
22 Muller Street
Yeoville 2198
Johannesburg, South Africa

ISBN
0-89906-574-0 (hard cover)

Typography by Compuscribe at ArtScroll Studios, Ltd.
4401 Second Avenue / Brooklyn, N.Y. 11232 / (718) 921-9000

Printed in the United States of America by
EDISON LITHOGRAPHING AND PRINTING CORP.
Bound by Sefercraft Quality Bookbinders, Ltd., Brooklyn, N.Y.

Contents

↪§ Authors' Preface

Speak to a boy after his *bar mitzvah*. Ask him what was the biggest surprise of his celebration. Chances are that he will tell you how unprepared he was that everything seemed to happen so fast. "I prepared for a whole year and in a few hours the whole thing was over," is a common post-*bar mitzvah* refrain. It's more than likely that parents feel the same way. So much work. . .so much preparation. . .over so soon.

I suppose the production of this book has left RABBI YONAH WEINRIB and myself with similar sentiments. Preparation beyond expectation. Information exceeding our original plan. However, just as the *bar mitzvah* boy is told that it is only the *celebration* that has ended so soon, but his labor will continue to bear fruit, our hope is the same. While the production of this book has been completed, our fervent prayer is that the information and inspiration that the readers may derive is only now beginning. True, the effort has been enormous, but so is the satisfaction. Our thanks to God is abundant.

The task of creating this book required the involvement of many people. Indeed, the list of well-deserved acknowledgements resembles the long invitation lists of many *bar mitzvah* celebrations. The finished product is a testimony to all those who believed in the significance of this project and its potential for illuminating the many dimensions of this pivotal event in a child's life לְהַגְדִיל תּוֹרָה וּלְהַאֲדִירָה. . ., *that the Torah be made great and glorious.*

Having been privileged to collaborate with RABBI YONAH WEINRIB on past projects of smaller scope, I am only now beginning to appreciate the varied talents of this humble man who masks his great skills and exemplary character. It is he who first envisioned the importance, and feasibility of producing this book, and whose perseverance assured that it would become a reality. The artwork in this volume is but a small sample of his vast portfolio of musical, written and artistic expressions — all directed and perfected toward one purpose — to be מְקַדֵּשׁ שֵׁם שָׁמַיִם בָּרַבִּים, *to publicly sanctify the Holy Name of God.*

In addition to writing the chapters on Allusions and *Bas Mitzvah*, R' Yonah's erudition and guiding hand can be felt on every page. It was only because of his commitments to countless other projects of equal import, that I was fortunate enough to be asked to help him realize this vision. I will forever be grateful to him for granting me this opportunity, and hope that I will continue to benefit from his and his sterling wife Miriam's שתחי׳ many efforts on behalf of their fellow Jews. May he continue to grow in his quest to fulfill King Solomon's charge כַּבֵּד אֶת ה׳ מֵהוֹנֶךָ, *Honor God with all your talents* (Proverbs 3:9).

RABBI HERSH GOLDWURM, the outstanding Torah scholar, reviewed the manuscript for halachic accuracy and fidelity to the sources. In addition, he reviewed and commented on the entire manuscript. Thanks to his attention to clarity and detail, the material presented herein was vastly improved. I am especially appreciative of the personal knowledge I gained from him, in advancing my understanding of the halachic process. The involvement of so outstanding a *talmid chacham* in this work is a source of great pride to us all.

More than anyone else, RABBI YOSEF GLATSTEIN helped me find the most lucid and precise way to communicate my thoughts throughout this book. For that reason it is difficult for me to adequately articulate my gratitude to him. R' Yossi's breadth of scholarship and coherent thought process is surpassed only by his devotion in sharing his knowledge with others. His contribution here was enormous.

Rare is the individual whose vibrancy and integrity are so great that they transcend generational barriers. RABBI PAYSACH KROHN is such a man. Besides his expertise in circumcision, Rabbi Krohn has the uncanny capacity to touch and teach audiences of *all* ages, through his renowned books and speeches. How appropriate that this work on *bar mitzvah,* marking the ascendance from childhood to adulthood, should benefit from his enormous skills. It is hard to measure how much his editorial direction and daily support meant to this project and to me.

I have been most fortunate to be able to have mentors such as RABBI AVRAHAM PAM, שליט״א, RABBI DAVID COHEN, שליט״א, and RABBI HILLEL DAVID, שליט״א, my *rav.*

Their sage counsel, encyclopedic knowledge, and warm encouragement have made an indelible impression on my family and me during the past two decades. Directly and indirectly, they have helped shape this book. I am greatly indebted to them.

Several existing books on *bar mitzvah* and related topics have contributed to my research and writing. Most notably are the works

by RABBI BINYAMIN ADLER, *Hilchos V'Halichos Bar Mitzvah*, RABBI
SHIMON EIDER, *Hilchos Tefillin, and* RABBI ISAAC RIVKIND, ע״ה, *Le'os
U'lezikaron*. Other authors whose books were helpful include RABBI
ARON ZAKKAI, RABBI DOVID MEISELS, RABBI NACHMAN COHEN, and RABBI
HERBERT DOBRINSKY. I am grateful to them all.

For the chapter on *bar mitzvah* customs I interviewed many
authorities, all of whom were very generous with their time and
information. I thank them all: RABBI YAAKOV PERLOW, RABBI NAFTALI
HALBERSTAM, RABBI ZECHARIAH GELLEY, RABBI DOVID MEISELS, RABBI
YECHEZKIEL KORNFELD, RABBI CHANANIAH ELBAZ, RABBI CHAIM YAAKOV
RUBIN, RABBI MORDECHAI COHEN, RABBI YITZCHAK ISAAC HANDLER, and
RABBI BERISH MANDELBAUM.

The suggestions and inquiries of my fellow *chavrei kollel* in
Yeshivah Torah Vodaath expanded the scope of this book and gave
me great support and encouragement. They include RABBIS LABEL
WULLIGER, DOVID STAM, YISRAEL REISMAN, MOTI KARFIOL, AVIGDOR
FEINTUCH, HESHY WOLF, MOSHE LAMM, and YONI LEVINSON. Their efforts
are greatly appreciated.

DR. MEIR WIKLER, therapist, author, mentor, and dearest friend, lent
his usual support and enthusiasm to this project. There is nothing I do
that does not carry his mark in some way. I am privileged and
thankful.

I am also grateful to RABBI YAAKOV LUBAN for allowing us use of a
drasha, discourse, for the *Pshet'l* section.

RABBI MESHULEM FEISH GINSBURG and R' DANIEL SUKENIK contributed
valuable stories for the Profiles section. Thank you both.

Many parents offer their children the necessary encouragement
and obligatory words of support for a project or venture. Few actually
roll up their sleeves and demonstrate their interest and concern. My
mother, MRS. LEA SALOMON, שתחי' knows no other way. Her keen
perception and relentless striving for clarity have had a profound
influence on my gestalt in life, my writing in general, and this book in
particular. Confusing or inconsistent nuances in the manuscript,
overlooked by others, could not slip past her discerning eye. She and
my father, R' TOVIA SALOMON, ע״ה taught me never to be satisfied with
anything less than my best effort. Any credit due me belongs to them.

The final and most heartfelt tribute belongs to my wife Temmy,
שתחי'. Behind me in every undertaking, beside me through every
waking hour, and well beyond me in character, sensitivity, perseverance, and *bitachon,* belief, her guiding hand has become my beacon

of confidence and anchor of support. With her own special brand of modesty and self-effacement, traits acquired from her dear parents, RABBI and MRS. ARON STERNBERG, she has quietly embedded an everlasting enthusiasm and sense of purpose on myself and all our children, שיחיו. Without her spiritual conviction and unwavering resolve, few, if any, of my aspirations would ever reach fruition. May Hashem grant us the privilege of seeing our children grow in Torah and *Yiras Shamayim*.

Yaakov Salomon

Elul 5751 / August 1991

❈ ❈ ❈

The artist's perceptions of an event, a concept or an object are colored by his feelings and experiences; the shades and hues that finally become the painted form reflect his personal perspectives.

In this sense, the challenge of a Judaica artist is to create more than just art on a Jewish theme. He must imbue the artwork with his Judaism, making his faith no less an integral component than his pigments and dyes. Artistic and creative talents are a gift from the Master Artist, given to man to be honed and refined, and hopefully rechanneled in His service. Thus, the challenge of this volume was to create artwork which would aesthetically enhance the text yet still reflect the richness of *bar mitzvah* and Jewish tradition.

For INGEBORG and IRA RENNERT, the *bar mitzvah* of their son ARI will have a profound impact far beyond the day he turns thirteen. By dedicating this volume, bringing the laws, customs and insights of the *bar mitzvah* to the English speaking public, they will add immeasurably to the *simchah* of thousands of others, for years to come. Our prayer to God is that by illuminating the concept of *bar mitzvah* through this book, we may share in the dissemination of His Torah.

The taxing pace and arduous hours invested in bringing the *bar mitzvah* book to fruition were made much more bearable by my collaboration with RABBI YAAKOV SALOMON. Our friendship of over twenty years is beautifully reflected in this project. R' Yaakov, a master craftsman in his own right, skillfully draws upon his storehouse of talents, energies, and abilities to execute to perfection every project he undertakes. As a colleague, mentor, and role model, R' Yaakov has demonstrated through private practice and public example the resolve to predicate his life and that of his family on the ultimate foundation of Torah — true priorities. I am privileged to share the valued friendship of this rare individual whom so many people consider their *yedid nefesh.*

With this project, my association with the ArtScroll family takes on a new dimension. My sincerest appreciation and admiration goes to RABBI MEIR ZLOTOWITZ, who helped me appreciate the pursuit of excellence in striving to present the treasures of Torah in a setting worthy of its beauty. The ArtScroll Series has truly become a present-day Sanctuary from which Torah and Godliness are disseminated; R' Meir is surely its Bezalel.

My years at ArtScroll Printing Corporation with ELLIOT and DAVID SCHWARTZ have been invaluable in gaining a sharper perspective on many aspects of production and creative design. Through their innovations, they have made ArtScroll the standard against which all others are judged.

The content and direction of my artwork reflects the influence of my *rebbeim* and teachers more than that of my art instructors. I am eternally grateful for the profound impact of RAV SHMUEL BRUDNY, ז״ל and RAV CHAIM SHMULEWITZ, ז״ל, two Torah giants, who, by virtue of their greatness, helped our generation see the heights that man can reach. The accessibility of RAV DAVID COHEN, שליט״א and RAV HILLEL DAVID, שליט״א, for their illuminating comments on my work is greatly appreciated, as their sensitivity enables them to view artwork through the prism of Torah. My *roshei yeshivah, rebbeim,* and colleagues at Mirrer Yeshiva and Agudath Israel *Snif Zichron Shmuel* have helped create the Torah environment in which many of my ideas were born. I am particularly grateful to my *rav,* RAV ELIEZER GINSBURG, שליט״א and RAV SHMUEL YOSEF LERCHER, שליט״א as well as dear friends and study partners R' SHMUEL DANZIGER and R' ZEVI TRENK for their support and encouragement. Special thanks to my brother-in-law, RABBI YITZCHOK ISBEE and also to RABBI JACOB J. SCHACTER for their contributions and comments. The able assistance of RANDY BARLIN is greatly appreciated.

Mention must be made of those patrons of the Jewish arts, people of vision who are partners in many of my works. If the works they commissioned have helped add some measure of beauty or visual excitement to the world, they can certainly share in the joy of that experience.

DEBBIE and ELLIOT GIBBER helped bring a dream to fulfillment by commissioning the Hebrew and Hebrew/English editions of the

Manuscript Shiron, a section of which is included at the end of this volume. The Manuscript Megillah on *Megillas Esther* afforded me the opportunity to add another artistic interpretation to this oft-illustrated text.

HELENE and ZYG WOLLOCH, for whom I completed the calligraphy and commentary of the *Haggadah* in Memory of the Holocaust together with DAVID WANDER, created a millieu in which to explore two poignant events in our history.

Pirkei Avos, Ethics of the Fathers, has been a labor of love for the past three years. NAOMI and HARVEY WOLINETZ, who commissioned the work to mark the *bar mitzvah* of their son, join me in the hope that the published edition will be another beautiful gem in the crown of God's Torah.

A special note of appreciation and thanks is due my wonderful parents and in-laws. To my parents, MR. and MRS. CHAIM WEINRIB, שיחיו, words can't adequately express the feelings for those who survived the tortures of Europe to rebuild a new life, predicated on self-sacrifice for others — and with a firm resolve to see beauty in every day that God grants. My in-laws, RABBI and MRS. LEIB ISBEE, שיחיו, have taught hundreds of students and congregants over a lifetime of service, but their best lesson was that which was imparted to their children by their example.

My eternal debt is to my wife, MIRIAM, 'שתחי, an active partner in all my undertakings, a constant source of support and encouragement in every project. May it be the will of Hashem that we continue to work together to create the Torah environment in our home for our children שיחיו, and that it radiates outward for the benefit of others. May each work be a song of praise to our Creator, and may we always be worthy of being brushes in the Hands of God.

Yonah Weinrib

Elul 5751 / August 1991

❧ ❧ ❧

It is indeed a privilege for both of us to have worked with the ArtScroll staff on this project. Exacting in their craftsmanship and uncompromising in their standards, the ArtScroll imprint is indelibly ingrained in this endeavor. Our profound thanks to RABBI MEIR ZLOTOWITZ for his overall direction and to RABBI NOSSON SCHERMAN for his insightful comments, literary assistance and critique. RABBI HERSH GOLDWURM was an invaluable resource for clarity of thought and halachic precision. We are also privileged to have benefitted from the editorial expertise of RABBI AVIE GOLD and RABBI YOSEF GESSER. The beauty of this volume was greatly enhanced by RABBI SHEAH BRANDER, designer par-excellence whose creative innovations are a hallmark of Mesorah Publications. Special thanks to his capable staff, YITZCHOK SAFTLAS, ELI KROEN, EPHRAIM ROSENSTOCK, BASSIE GOLDSTEIN, NICHIE FENDRICH, MRS. JUDI DICK, and most notably, YEHUDA GORDON for their technical assistance on behalf of this publication.

Yaakov Salomon
Yonah Weinrib

Wimpel

A wimpel, the German-Yiddish word for the Torah binder, was often embroidered by Ashkenazic Jews to be used as swaddling clothes for a male child's circumcision. It was dedicated upon the child's first visit to the synagogue or a similar festive occasion. The text embroidered on the wimpel is taken from the bris milah service, and the child's name and birthdate were often included. "Just as he entered the covenant (of Abraham), so may he enter into the study of Torah, the marriage canopy and a life of good deeds" (Shabbos 137b). Ashkenazic wimpeln often contained pictorial representations of the text, while Sephardic Torah binders of Italy and Turkey had elaborate floral motifs and patterns.

Scripture places special significance on the role of chinuch, training a child in the ways and commandments of the Torah in his youth, to prepare him for their performance when he becomes obligated as a bar mitzvah. From the time he enters the Covenant of Abraham at his bris milah the child is imbued with a love for God's Torah and Jewish ritual.

OVERVIEW-
FOUNDATIONS FOR
THE FUTURE

An Overview —
Foundations For The Future

There is no greater festive meal in commemoration of a mitzvah than that which is tendered to give praise and thanksgiving to God that a child has been privileged to become bar mitzvah . . . and his parent has been privileged to raise him to this point and to bring him into the covenant of the Torah (Yam shel Shlomo, Bava Kamma 87:37).

ar or *bas mitzvah* is the first major milestone in the life of a Jewish youngster, and a major milestone it is. The new assumption of responsibility to perform the commandments as an adult should carry with it an awareness of the hurdles to be surmounted along the road of life, and the God-given ability to accomplish great things. That is sufficient cause for celebration. Parents rejoice and call their dear ones to celebrate with them when a child is born; in a real sense, that same child is reborn when he or she attains religious majority. And that, too, is cause for celebration.

Life needs the stimulation of such milestones. We need times that make us stop and take stock of ourselves and our lives, of our past and future, of our potential and aspiration. It is sad, therefore, that in modern times, particularly in affluent Western society, the underlying purpose of the *bar mitzvah* has come to be overshadowed by a frenetic preoccupation with the ceremony and celebration, the pomp of the dinner, and the accumulation of gifts.

Life needs the stimulation of such milestones. We need times that make us stop and take stock of ourselves.

If only there was a realization that the greatest gift is the significance of the day and what it brings into the life of the boy or girl who has crossed over into young adulthood! But that concept is often buried in the clutter of preparation. When it is over, there may not be anything tangible to mark the event as a threshold that has been crossed. The new "man" or "woman" has not changed addresses or schools. They have not grown an inch, gained a pound, or added a point to their I.Q. scores. What, then, does the *bar mitzvah* represent and what should the new "adult" and his parents retain when the festivities are over?

The greatest gift is the significance of the day and what it brings into the life of the boy or girl

I. Rashness and Responsibility

An Act of War

The ages of thirteen for *bar mitzvah* and twelve for *bas mitzvah* were given to Moses at Sinai as part of the Oral Law (*Rashi* to *Pirkei Avos* 5:21; *Teshuvos HaRosh* 16:1). However, the commentators find Scriptural allusions to the age of thirteen, and it is from those verses that we can begin to understand the goals that should impel the *bar mitzvah* as he moves onward from his first great milestone.

The first of these verses describes a deed that was carried out by two of Jacob's sons, when they had just passed their *bar mitzvah* age.

,,וַיִּקְחוּ שְׁנֵי־בְנֵי־יַעֲקֹב שִׁמְעוֹן וְלֵוִי אֲחֵי דִינָה אִישׁ חַרְבּוֹ. . .

Two of Jacob's sons, Simeon and Levi, Dinah's brothers, each took his sword. . ." (Genesis 34:25).

It was one of the most dangerous periods in the lifetime of Jacob and his young family. His daughter Dinah had been abducted and ravished by Shechem, the crown prince of the Canaanite city that bore his name. The criminal then had the gall to come with his father to "negotiate" with Jacob and his sons. They proposed that the Canaanites and Israelites would become brothers in marriage and commerce, and Dinah would remain Shechem's "princess," whether or not she desired the honor. Jacob's sons duped the Shechemites into circumcising themselves, and then Simeon and Levi rescued their sister by single-handedly waging war and wiping out the entire male population of the offending city.

Simeon and Levi rescued their sister by single-handedly waging war.

Jacob criticized them sharply for their action, for they had made the entire family the potential target of avenging Canaanites. Simeon and Levi did not respond directly to his practical criticism. They said merely "הַכְזוֹנָה יַעֲשֶׂה אֶת אֲחוֹתֵנוּ, *should he treat our sister as a harlot?!"* (ibid. 34:31)

They had been outraged. Their sister had been mistreated and they could not tolerate it!

Logically, Jacob was right, but they had not acted out of logic. They had been outraged. Their sister had been mistreated and they could not tolerate it! [See comm. to ArtScroll *Genesis* for a full discussion of the justification for the brothers' deed.]

Future Destiny

Jacob's anger at their rashness was not a temporary phenomenon. Half a century later, as he lay on his deathbed and gave his blessings to his children, Jacob expressed his ire at Simeon and Levi, saying,

Accursed is their rage for it is fierce, and their wrath for it is

18 □ BAR MITZVAH

harsh; I will separate them within Jacob, and I will disperse them within Israel (*ibid* 49:7).

As the Midrash explains, Jacob recognized that if Simeon and Levi were to be neighbors, they would again influence one another to engage in rash and destructive conduct, with potentially disastrous results for themselves and the nation. Jacob wanted them to be separated permanently and to be kept away from positions of political power. Therefore he ordained that they be separated and dispersed. Neither tribe had a contiguous share of Eretz Yisrael; the Levites had forty-eight scattered cities and the Simeonites share of the land was sprinkled throughout the southern portion of Judah's province.

But it was not only their territory, or lack of it, that kept them from power. Their means of livelihood, too, kept them from dominion. Simeon's offspring were poor people — scribes and elementary school teachers — the sort who would be required to depend on others for their livelihood. The Levites and the *Kohanim*, who descended from Levi, would depend on the tithes and priestly gifts for their sustenance, so that they would be forced to travel from farm to farm to collect the gifts. Clearly, the Simeonites and Levites were doomed to an economic and political second class-status.

Jacob wanted them to be separated permanently and to be kept away from positions of political power.

If we look more deeply, however, we will see that for all his annoyance with them, Jacob gave Simeon and Levi an elevated status, indeed. The Levites were the spiritual elite of the nation. The Simeonites, as teachers, would have a pivotal influence on all Israel. Is this influential role the one Jacob wanted for the tribes he criticized in such strong terms? Yes. Jacob balanced his treatment of the two tribes, so that their brethren would gain from their virtues while being shielded from their vices.

A Necessary Trait

Their brethren would gain from their virtues while being shielded from their vices.

By curtailing their temporal power, Jacob prevented them from ever again leading Israel into rash and dangerous adventures. But their motives for attacking Shechem had not escaped his notice — or admiration. They had refused to tolerate the victimization of their sister. Should he treat our sister as a harlot?! Alone among their brothers, they had endangered themselves to save her. This devotion to brethren was a trait that Jacob wished to encourage, not for the sake of rewarding Simeon and Levi, but to elevate the rest of the tribes by teaching them that Israel was a united, intertwined nation, and that no Jew should feel secure while another is suffering. So the two tribes that had incurred his wrath became the teachers and role

This devotion to brethren was a trait that Jacob wished to encourage.

models of the people. Let Israel know that its intermediaries in the Temple and the priests in its temples of education would come from the two brothers who refused to remain calm in the face of outrage against Dinah (*R' Yosef Kimchi; Haamek Davar; Malbim*).

In describing their aggressive attack against the Shechemites, the Torah identifies Simeon and Levi as the brothers of Dinah, because they refused to set aside their brotherly feelings in the interests of personal safety. And it refers to them with the term איש, man (*Genesis* 34:25). The commentators note that Levi, the younger of the two, was thirteen years old at the time. This alludes to the age of *bar mitzvah* because the Torah suggests that boys who had reached the age of thirteen could be called men.

In describing their aggressive attack against the Shechemites, the Torah refers to them with the term איש, man.

Let us go a step further. It is fair to say that in alluding to the status of Simeon and Levi, the Torah refers not only to the chronological age of majority, but also to the mission it entails. People are called men when they prove that they are ready to act on behalf of others; when they demonstrate a sense of responsibility for their fellow Jews. Indeed, Jacob wedded the destiny of those brothers to this concept of brotherhood.

II. Israel's Mission

Word and Deed

There is another verse that alludes to the age of *bar mitzvah*:

"עַם זוּ יָצַרְתִּי לִי תְּהִלָּתִי יְסַפֵּרוּ"

This nation have I fashioned for myself that it shall declare My praise (Isaiah 43:21).

The word זוּ, *this*, has the numerical value of 13 [*zayin* = 7; *vav* = 6], thus alluding to the age at which a minor becomes a part of his people's destiny. That destiny is to declare the praise of God, in deed as well as in word (*Orchos Chaim; Midrash Shmuel*).

As Moses said over and over in *Deuteronomy*, his last words to the Jewish people, they were to conduct themselves in such a way that whoever saw them would recognize the Godliness that they carried upon them. These praises that Jews are to express to God are hardly limited to the synagogue or the study hall. When a Jew at the playground or the office acts in such a way that onlookers say "This is the nation of God," he has proclaimed the praise of his Maker.

The Jewish people, were to conduct themselves in such a way that whoever saw them would recognize the Godliness that they carried.

This writer was once told by Rabbi Yaakov Kamenetsky that shortly after he became rabbi of Tzitivyan, he mailed a letter from the local one-man post office. The postmaster gave him too much change and, after he counted it and detected the error, Reb Yaakov gave back the extra money. The postmaster smiled slyly, and Reb Yaakov was convinced that he had been testing the new Jewish "rabbin" to see if he was honest. During World War II, that postmaster helped save Jews from the Nazis, and Reb Yaakov always felt that his own performance when his honesty was being scrutinized may have had a bearing on the man's behavior during the war. Who knows? But one thing is certain: those moments in the post office of an insignificant Russian hamlet were one Jew's opportunity to declare God's greatness. He was given his chance to fulfill his personal mission of praising God through his deeds. Reb Yaakov met the challenge.

Those moments in the post office of an insignificant Russian hamlet were one Jew's opportunity to declare God's greatness.

The particular responsibility to be a living declaration of the Divine image comes upon a Jewish child when he or she crosses the threshold of *bar mitzvah*. *Sfas Emes* addressed this theme at the *bar mitzvah* of one of his sons. He cited the reference in the Midrash referring to Jacob and Esau coming of age:

Invigorating the Organs

> And the lads [i.e., Jacob and Esau] grew up (*Genesis 25:27*). R' Pinchas said in the name of R' Levi: They were like a myrtle and a rose bush growing next to one another. When they become mature, one becomes fragrant and the other produces thorns. For thirteen years, [both Jacob and Esau] went to the study hall and returned home. Thereafter, only one went to the study hall, while the other went to places of idolatry (*Bereishis Rabbah 63:10*).

Before their *bar mitzvah*, there may be no noticeable difference between a Jacob and an Esau. The difference begins to become apparent when a Jewish child becomes *bar mitzvah* and receives the potential of enhanced spirituality. For the Sages teach that when God created man, He fashioned the *yetzer hatov* and the *yetzer hara*, the Good Inclination and the Evil Inclination. They teach further that the Good Inclination comes at the age of *bar mitzvah*. This is simultaneous with the new "adult's" responsibility to begin observing all the commandments on his own, independent of the parental responsibility of training and education.

The Good Inclination comes at the age of bar mitzvah.

Since, according to the well-known teaching, the 613 commandments correspond to the 613 primary limbs, organs, and blood vessels, a new spiritual dimension is added to a person when he assumes his religious majority and becomes obligated to perform the commandments. Each *mitzvah* gives life to its corresponding bodily

Without the performance of the required commandments the body is spiritually starved and may even die a spiritual death.

part, just as the soul gives life to the body as a whole. Without the performance of the required commandments — or the study of the laws of those commandments whose performance may be impossible — the body is spiritually starved and may even die a spiritual death.

This concept is hardly as esoteric as it may seem at first blush. Modern society is plagued by huge multitudes of people who have been so deprived of love, education, and what have always been considered basic moral teachings, that society is almost at war with itself. Terms like underclass and drug culture have been coined to describe groups that are so far from the prevailing morality that they are virtually a different human species. Is it so difficult in such a context to speak of a spiritual death while a person thrives physically?

Is it so difficult to speak of a spiritual death while a person thrives physically.

A Second Birth

This phenomenon of a spiritual infusion at the age of *bar mitzvah* indicates a profound change in a person. In a real sense, it is like a second birth: a newborn baby achieves physical life; the *bar mitzvah* a new spiritual life. He or she has become the Jew for whom the world was created. In a related sense, he or she has assumed a personal responsibility to carry out the mission for which man was created and Israel chosen. The body is the external creation; the soul, as represented by the Good Inclination and the performance of commandments, is the internal creation.

There are three partners in man: his mother, his father, and God. Though each contributes an indispensable part to the human being, it should not be surprising that the share of each comes to its primary fruition at different stages of a person's existence. In the physical sense, this is obvious. Psychologically, too, a growing child changes its dependence from mother to father as it grows older. Spiritually, too, *Sfas Emes* expounds, *bar/bas mitzvah* is a time when a boy or girl is created anew, when they begin the task of developing their primary allegiance to God's mission, and becoming a living orchestra that plays the symphony of His praise. A young person changes when he becomes the host to a new life-long companion, the Good Inclination, which can transform him into the throne upon which God's presence reveals itself on earth.

Spiritually, bar/bas mitzvah is a time when a boy or girl is created anew, when they begin the task of developing their primary allegiance to God's mission.

Fashioning Sanctity

To this concept, one may add that the Tabernacle in the Wilderness, the forerunner of the Holy Temple in Jerusalem and God's dwelling place on earth, was built under the direction of

Bezalel, who was then only thirteen years old. In choosing him for this august task, perhaps God was demonstrating that just as Bezalel and his co-workers were bringing Godliness into more noticeable proximity to earth, so, too, every person who becomes *bar mitzvah* must build his personal tabernacle within himself.

As noted above, it is at the age of thirteen, when he assumes the responsibility for the commandments, that a boy is called אִישׁ, *a man*. So, too, at the age of twelve a girl becomes אִשָּׁה, *a woman*. In illustrating the sanctity of marriage, the Talmud teaches that the letter *yud* of the man and the letter *hei* of the woman combine to spell a Name of God. Indeed, God used the letters of that Name to create heaven and earth. The use of these letters in אִישׁ וְאִשָּׁה, the terms indicating religious majority, are no accident. As we have seen, boys and girls achieve a new spiritual status when they become *bar/bas mitzvah*. This is a new creation, and it is worthy of the same joy that parents and loved ones feel when a new baby is born. Rabbi Avraham Mordechai Alter of Gur once put it wittily: Whenever a Jewish child becomes a *bar mitzvah*, it is cause for general joy. Just as a borrower is happy when he finds someone to co-sign on his loan, so, too, every new Jewish adult is a guarantor for the entire nation.

III. Product of the Past

The very term *bar mitzvah* sheds light on the significance of the day, to the child and to his or her parents. Wouldn't it have been more logical to simply use a word that means adult, such as *gadol* and *gedolah*? And why do we use the Aramaic *bar* for "son," instead of the Hebrew *ben*?

It has been suggested that in the context of *bar mitzvah*, the word *bar* is not the Aramaic word for son. Rather it is the Hebrew word בַּר, which means grain or produce [see *Genesis* 42:25, et al.].

Grain does not grow spontaneously. It requires seeding, plowing, watering, weeding, and so on. It demands sincere and fervent prayer, because all of man's efforts may be wasted if God does not cause nature to cooperate. When the crop finally appears and is harvested, everyone knows that it did not appear in a vacuum.

So, too, is the child who attains majority. He is a product of his parents, his surroundings, his education, his upbringing. He is literally בַּר מִצְוָה, *the product of the commandments*, as the commandments have been practiced by those who nurtured him and as he has been raised to love and perform them. There is never a guarantee that the

There is no substitute for the example and sincerity of mothers and fathers whose goals are clear and who show their love.

most strenuous and sincere efforts of parents will bear the sort of fruit they tried to plant; even Isaac and Rebecca produced an Esau. But there is no substitute for the example and sincerity of mothers and fathers whose goals are clear and who show their love by knowing when to say yes and when to say no, and not being afraid to do so.

Lasting Foundations

It is easy to dismiss the deeds and aspirations of boys and girls, even after their *bar mitzvah*, as being no more than a preparation for the "real thing," when they are more mature. This is a drastically mistaken attitude. *Arizal* notes that God said to the Jewish people:

„זָכַרְתִּי לָךְ חֶסֶד נְעוּרַיִךְ אַהֲבַת כְּלוּלֹתָיִךְ לֶכְתֵּךְ אַחֲרַי בַּמִּדְבָּר בְּאֶרֶץ
לֹא זְרוּעָה,

I remember for your sake the kindness of your youth, the love of your bridal days, how you followed Me in the Wilderness in an unsown land" (Jeremiah 2:2).

That prophecy referred to the first few weeks after the Exodus, when the people were marching from Egypt on their way to Sinai. They had left the cradle of civilization and gone, as the verse states, to an unsown wasteland, where there was no food, water, or housing. God reckoned this devoted faith as a "kindness" done Him by Israel, an expression of the sort of unselfish love that newlyweds feel for one another.

God reckoned this devoted faith as a "kindness" done Him by Israel.

That total devotion to God was weakened soon after when the people worshiped the Golden Calf. Eight centuries later, the nation had sinned so grievously for so long that it was on the verge of the destruction of the First Temple and the Babylonian Exile. It was far, far from the kindness, love, and loyalty of those glorious days on the way to Sinai. Nevertheless, God still remembered fondly the early days of Israel's greatness, days which should have long since faded into oblivion.

When foundations are strong, they can be used again, even after the building has been badly damaged.

Those early weeks never lost their significance because during those few dozen days the nation laid the foundation for its eternal status as God's Chosen People. Such is the importance of a proper beginning. When foundations are strong, they can be used again, even after the building has been badly damaged, or even destroyed.

Arizal likens every individual Jew to the nation of Israel. Every Jew is the product of his youth, for that is when his personal foundation is set in place. He may -- and almost certainly will — flounder very often as he goes through life. So did Israel — but God remembered and still remembers those fundamental weeks, though they ended so soon. The impression remained. Fall though it might, the nation that had begun so auspiciously had established a plateau to which it could climb again. So, too, the individual. Young and immature? Yes, but so was Israel. Nevertheless, the early years of personal growth from the *bar mitzvah* onward are pattern-setting times. The later decades of life and achievement may well rest upon the innocence and enthusiasm of such youthful aspiration.

The early years of personal growth from the bar mitzvah onward are pattern-setting times.

Fall You Must

In response to a student who had written of his disappointment in what he saw as his lack of success in his studies, Rabbi Yitzchok Hutner wrote a warm, perceptive, and inspiring letter that should be required reading for all youngsters and their educators (*Pachad Yitzchak, Igros U'Kesavim* p. 217). The following concepts are extracted from that letter:

> There is a mistaken and damaging tendency to focus on our great Torah leaders in their mature years. In so doing, we skip their years of struggle to become great; it is as if they emerged from the womb as accomplished scholars and tzaddikim. We marvel at the Chafetz Chaim's purity of speech, but who knows about his battles to tame the normal Evil Inclination, of the inevitable struggles and defeats that are part of growth and advancement? . . . Know, my beloved, that the root of your soul is not in the tranquility of your Good Inclination, but specifically in the war against the Evil Inclination. Your worthy and heartfelt letter testifies like a hundred witnesses that you are a loyal warrior in the ranks of the Good Inclination. In English the saying goes "lose a battle and win the war." Surely you have failed and you will fail again . . . and on many fronts you will fall wounded. But I assure you that after the loss of all the battles, you will emerge from the war with the crown of victory on your head . . . The wisest of all men said, The righteous man will fall seven times, but will arise (*Proverbs* 24:16). Fools think that this means . . . even though he will fall, nevertheless, he will rise. Wise men know well that the intent is [the opposite:] that the nature of the *tzaddik's* rise is *because* of his "seven downfalls."

There is a mistaken and damaging tendency to focus on our great Torah leaders in their mature years.

Wise men know that the nature of the tzaddik's rise is because of his "seven downfalls."

Failure is not the enemy of success; it is its prerequisite. Do not think that great men and their Good Inclinations are inseparable

Failure is not the enemy of success; it is its prerequisite.

as Siamese twins. Great people were not born; they were made. They made themselves great through desire and effort — and by failing, but learning from their failures and refusing to submit to them.

Welcome

As a Jewish child crosses the threshold of the commandments, his people welcomes him, and his God awaits him happily with a wealth of spiritual potential. His world is open. More, he can fashion his world and make it a sound foundation for future accomplishment. It is indeed a happy time and one worthy of celebration, but the trappings of joy should not obscure the reason for joy. If one can make that distinction, then his *bar mitzvah* will truly be an auspicious event, for himself, his family, his people, and his world.

Rabbi Nosson Scherman

Elul 5751 / August 1991

As a Jewish child crosses the threshold of the commandments, his world is open. More, he can fashion his world.

A MESSAGE
TO THE
BAR MITZVAH BOY

A Message to the Bar Mitzvah Boy

The calendar date has long ago been circled. The anticipation has been building for many months. Maybe even years! The plans have been discussed, debated, finalized, altered, and finalized again. Soon the long wait will finally be over. Your *bar mitzvah* is here.

The commotion, preparation and exertion for THE EVENT is unlike anything you've ever witnessed before. And yet, you're probably troubled by one major question. "Why?"

The question is a good one. After all, you learned Torah before your *bar mitzvah* and you will learn Torah after your *bar mitzvah*. You observed the *Sabbath* and ate *matzoh* on Passover before your *bar mitzvah*, and you'll do the same after your *bar mitzvah*. How will one day make a difference? Does something magical occur overnight that suddenly transforms every *mitzvah*, every action you take?

The answer can probably be best understood by reflecting on an observation once made by Irving Bunim ע״ה, noted Torah supporter and philosopher. Speaking at a *bar mitzvah* celebration, he wondered why it is that our Sages said that a boy reaches *bar mitzvah* age when he is thirteen years and one day. In fact, he is really a full-fledged *gadol,* halachic adult, when he is exactly thirteen years old?

His profound answer was that a boy becoming *bar mitzvah* must focus his attention on the day *after* the celebration is over. All *bar mitzvah* boys radiate sincerity and holiness on the day of their *bar mitzvah* — it's what happens afterwards that really counts!

The message is clear. Reaching *bar mitzvah* status is an enormous responsibility, but it is just the beginning of a lifetime of potential for growth and contribution.

Time is Life

When the eldest son of Rabbi Yaakov Kamenetsky זצ״ל became a bar mitzvah, he was summoned to his father's study. Reb Yaakov climbed onto a bench to reach for a carefully wrapped package and told his son, "Now that you are a bar mitzvah, I want to give you the most precious commodity in the world. You must promise me that you will guard it as your very life."

Reb Yaakov opened the package and presented his son with a wrist watch. He added, "Reb Yisrael Salanter would say that time is life; when time is wasted, a portion of one's life has actually been lost."

As you enter this awesome fraternity, you will quickly discover that your newly acquired responsibilities will affect three different relationships in life; you and God, you and the Jewish People, and finally, you and yourself.

Even before your father utters those dramatic four words: "בָּרוּךְ שֶׁפְּטָרַנִי מֵעָנְשׁוֹ שֶׁלָּזֶה, *Blessed is the One who has freed me from the punishment due this boy,*" you already will have embarked on a new stage of independence. The expectations that God now places on you to fulfill His *mitzvos*, commandments, is complete and unconditional. All those years of performing the *mitzvos bain adam l'makom*, between man and his Maker, and *bain adam l'chavero*, between man and his fellow man, were mere preparations for your life ahead. Every *shemoneh esrei* you ever davened, every quarter you dropped in a *pushka*, every moment that you resisted speaking *lashon hara*, slander, were prototypes of practice designated to prepare you for the REAL THING.

You and God

Those very same *mitzvos*, so familiar to you when you were younger, now carry with them newfound meaning and vast responsibility. Simply put, the exhibition games are over; the season begins.

You and the Jewish People

It won't take long for you to notice that people respond to you differently than they did before. What was yesterday called a "childish prank" is now seen as "immaturity" and "not befitting a *bar mitzvah* boy's behavior." What was previously looked at as "forgetfulness," is now called "negligence."

Somehow, from the moment a child is deemed responsible enough to care for valuable items like his own *tefillin*, he is perceived with a certain measure of respect and air of expectation. Like the uniform on the Army private or the stethoscope that dangles from the doctor's neck, the *tefillin* on the *bar mitzvah* boy and his capacity to perform adult functions for his fellow man, command a definite esteem and admiration.

Just look around. Practically every law and ritual that you will demonstrate in your *bar mitzvah* celebration, gives a communal message.

> "I can be called to the Torah. . . count me for a *minyan*."
> "I can deliver a *pshet'l*, sermon. . .I can teach others."
> "I can read from the Torah and be a *chazzan*. . .if leadership is needed, call me."

All these are designed to teach you that man's obligation is not only to God but to his family, his friends, his community. . .his people.

But the obligation does not stop there. The final link to the chain of *bar mitzvah* responsibility is your own accountability to yourself.

You and Yourself

Our *Chazal*, Sages, have taught us that upon your becoming a *bar mitzvah*, you are privileged to welcome a most honored partner in life — the *yetzer tov*, Good Inclination. After years of struggling valiantly on your own against the *yetzer hora*, Evil Inclination, help has finally arrived. But it is up to you to utilize it most efficiently.

Only you can gaze into the mirror and see yourself. Only you can judge if your utmost potential is being realized. And only you can face the daily tests and challenges of life and decide on the best route and destination. Yes. The responsibility is enormous, but so are the rewards. . .and the satisfaction.

It's true. The word that assumes newly pronounced significance when a boy reaches *bar mitzvah* age is obligation. Obligation on many different levels. But perhaps of equal importance is the emergence of another word — opportunity. Opportunity for reward. Opportunity for acceptance. Opportunity for fulfillment. And opportunities, in today's world of unprecedented technology and freedom, for unlimited growth — personally, communally and spiritually.

Yes. The calendar date was circled a long time ago. But the pages that follow it will be turned and discarded very quickly — never again to be retrieved. The future is truly in your hands. And it starts today!

INSIGHTS
and
aLLUSIONS

INSIGHTS דרש AND ALLUSIONS

hile the *bar mitzvah* is one of the most widely celebrated rituals in Judaism, there is no direct reference in the *Torah shebiksav*, the written Torah, to the exact age when one reaches adulthood and the obligation to observe the *mitzvos* begins. Later, we will outline some derivations made in the *Talmud* and *Midrash* on an *Aggadic* level. The Mishnah's statement: "A thirteen year old becomes obliged to observe the commandments" (*Avos*, 5:25) indicates that halachically one becomes an adult at that age. The change of status from a child who is neither obligated in *mitzvos* nor culpable for his transgressions, to an adult who is fully obligated and culpable, takes place when one reaches the age of thirteen years old and a day. This is a *halachah l'Moshe miSinai*, part of the oral tradition transmitted to Moshe at Sinai (*Rosh*, *Responsa* 16:1).

⋖§ The Term Bar Mitzvah

Does one *celebrate* a *bar mitzvah*, or does one *become* a *bar mitzvah*? While the term as it is used today often refers to the festive celebration of the event, according to traditional sources it generally refers to a state of being. One becomes a *bar mitzvah*, at the age of thirteen and one day. The term *bar* or *ben* is used in Aramaic or Hebrew to denote inclusion in a category. A *bar daas* is one who possesses the knowledge to perform certain Torah or Rabbinic actions; a *bar mitzvah* joins the fraternity of those who are obligated in commandments.

The usage of the term *bar mitzvah* is found in the Talmud (*Sanhedrin* 84b) where it differentiates between the *bar mitzvah*, who is obligated in the observance of the commandments and the minor,

The First *Mitzvah*
The first Scriptural mitzvah performed by a young man as he becomes thirteen is the recitation of the Shema. His involvement with the mitzvah begins with the pronouncement of the words הי אֱלֹקֵינוּ הי אֶחָד. *The numerical equivalent of* אֶחָד *is 13.*

— Shem MiShmuel

who is not. Generally, the Talmud distinguishes between a *katan*, a minor, less than thirteen years old, and a *gadol,* one who is older. Other terms used are *bar daas* or *ben daas*, referring to the level of acumen and understanding assumed to have been acquired by one who has reached thirteen.

The term is used in the period of the *Rishonim*, where they speak of the child not being subject to the death penalty "until he is *bar mitzvah*." (*Ibn Ezra, Leviticus* 20:7). Responsa during that period also refer to the obligation to perform one's own *pidyon haben*, redemption of the firstborn, when one becomes *bar mitzvah*, if his father died when he was less than thirty days old. (*Ohr Zarua* vol. I:514). A son replaces his father upon his death in regard to community matters "when he becomes a *bar mitzvah*." (*Rosh* Responsa 13:13).

Additionally, the thirteen year old has the appelation of *bar onshin*, one who is liable to receive punishment for his transgressions, now that he is part of the community of adults. 'In Italy, the newly achieved status of being considered of age for a quorum of ten, earned the young man the title *"min haminyan"* (*Le'os U'lezikaron, Rabbi Isaac Rivkind*, pg. 26).

The hallmark of one who has become a *gadol*, a halachic adult, is his measure of wisdom. While I.Q. and intellect are not determining factors, our Sages have made the age of thirteen the age of a man; a *gadol* has *daas*, wisdom; a *katan,* a minor, has no wisdom (*Yoma* 43a). The ramifications of not having "halachic wisdom" is that as precocious as the child may be, he cannot effect transactions, be liable in many legal matters or exempt an adult through his own performance of a *mitzvah.*

The celebration of the young man coming of age has taken various forms, from a simple *kiddush* to an exercise in opulent ostentation. The first reference to a *bar mitzvah* meal is the feast prepared by our Patriarch Abraham when Isaac was weaned. The *Midrash* (*Bereishis Rabbah* 53:10) tells us that this is a reference to being weaned from the *yetzer hara*, the Evil Inclination. Some commentators take this as a reference to Isaac's *bar mitzvah* (see *Peirush Maharsu*; cf. *Mishnas R'Eliezer* there). The *Customs* section will deal with a more extensive treatment of the *bar mitzvah* celebration.

Another title bestowed upon the *bar mitzvah* when he is called to the Torah for the first time is *habachur habar mitzvah*; the young man

Bar Mitzvah Bachur — Chasan HaBar Mitzvah

INSIGHTS AND aLLusions

who has become a *bar mitzvah*. In our morning prayers we recite the blessing "הַבּוֹחֵר בְּעַמּוֹ יִשְׂרָאֵל בְּאַהֲבָה, *He who chooses His people, Israel, with love.*" When a child reaches the age of *ahava*, the numerical equivalent of thirteen, he becomes a chosen member of God's beloved people (*Chasam Sofer*).

An additional title for one who reaches thirteen, is the term *chasan habar mitzvah*.

The word *chasan*, groom, makes reference to the fact that there is a similarity between the *bar mitzvah* boy and a groom on the day of his marriage. There is a *mitzvah* for a father to make a festive meal for his son when he becomes *bar mitzvah* as he would on the day that his son is brought under the marriage canopy (*Magen Avraham* 225:4). This halachic dictate is based on the actions of Rabbi Shimon bar Yochai, who prepared a lavish meal and decorated the house with beautiful ornaments on the day his son Elazar became *bar mitzvah*, "for on that day righteous people should rejoice as on the day one enters the *chupah*." (*Zohar Chadash* 11a). The joy, says the *Zohar*, becomes complete when the child reaches thirteen and he is responsible to follow the dictates of the Torah.

When one becomes a *bar mitzvah* he receives the legacy of Torah given to Moses. "תּוֹרָה צִוָּה לָנוּ מֹשֶׁה מוֹרָשָׁה, *Moses commanded us the Torah, which is a legacy*" (*Deuteronomy* 33:4). The *Talmud*, in a play on the word מוֹרָשָׁה, tells us to define it as מְאוֹרָסָה, *betrothed*. One who inherits the Torah legacy of Moses is like one who is betrothed (*Chasam Sofer, Genesis*).

The comparison of a *bar mitzvah* to a *chasan*, according to some, is more than a symbolic connection, but has practical halachic applications. The verse says: "כְּחָתָן יְכַהֵן פְּאֵר, *like a groom he will be adorned with splendor*" (*Isaiah* 61:10). *Tefillin* are also referred to as splendor. Just as we do not say *tachanun* in the presence of a *chasan*, so too, according to these opinions, we do not say *tachanun* when one becomes halachically obligated in *tefillin*, on the day of his *bar mitzvah* (*Nehar Mitzrayim* 6a). While this custom was practiced in Egypt, most have the custom to say *tachanun* on the day of one's *bar mitzvah* and when he dons *tefillin* for the first time. (See the *Customs* section for a more detailed discussion.)

INSIGHTS *אפרים ודיל* AND ALLUSIONS

❧ Bar Mitzvah — Why Thirteen?

While thirteen years old and one day is the point of entry into adult responsibility for a male, it is twelve years and one day for a female (*Niddah* 45b). The distinction is based on the Talmud's interpretation of the verse: "וַיִּבֶן ה' אֱלֹקִים אֶת הַצֵּלָע, *and God fashioned the rib*" (Genesis 2:22). The word וַיִּבֶן, also connotes בִּינָה, *understanding*, indicating that woman was created with a greater measure of insight and understanding than her male counterpart. Because her intellectual and emotional faculties develop more quickly than a young man's, her obligation to perform the *mitzvos* begins earlier as well (ibid.).

❧ "וַיִּגְדַּל הַיֶּלֶד וַיִּגָּמַל, *and the child grew and he was weaned*" (Genesis 21:8). The cause for the feast tendered by Abraham was that at that time Isaac became a *bar mitzvah*, weaned from his *yetzer hara*, *his Evil Inclination*. As mentioned earlier, some commentators say this refers to Isaac's *bar mitzvah* (*Bereishis Rabbah* 53:10).

❧ The Torah uses the term אִישׁ to denote a person who is fully responsible for observing all the positive and negative commandments (*Nazir* 29a). When Shechem, the son of Chamor abducted Dinah, the daughter of Jacob, Simeon and Levi, the two sons of Jacob, took their swords to exact revenge upon him and his city. The verse tells us: "וַיִּקְחוּ שְׁנֵי בְנֵי יַעֲקֹב שִׁמְעוֹן וְלֵוִי אֲחֵי דִינָה אִישׁ חַרְבּוֹ, *Two of Jacob's sons, Simeon and Levi Dinah's brothers, each took his sword*" (Genesis 34:25), referring to Simeon and Levi as אִישׁ. *Midrash Shmuel* and *Rashi* in *Nazir* 29a and in *Avos* calculate that they were thirteen at that time, and received the appelation of אִישׁ. (See Overview, page 18.)

❧ Bezalel, the primary architect of the *Mishkan*, the Tabernacle, was thirteen at the time of its construction (*Sanhedrin* 69b). The verse states: "אִישׁ אִישׁ מִמְּלַאכְתּוֹ, *each and every man from his work*" (Exodus 36:4). The use of אִישׁ in conjunction with this prodigious thirteen year old attests to the status of adulthood reached at that age. Scripture further ascribes wisdom and understanding, the hallmarks of adulthood, to Bezalel. "וָאֲמַלֵּא אֹתוֹ רוּחַ אֱלֹקִים בְּחָכְמָה וּבִתְבוּנָה וּבְדַעַת וּבְכָל מְלָאכָה, *And I filled him with the Spirit of God, with wisdom and with understanding and with knowledge and with all types of work" (Exodus 31:3).*

ـ§ Although a child is born with an Evil Inclination, his Good Inclination does not join him until he is thirteen (*Avos d' Rav Nosson*, chap. 16:2)[1].

ـ§ King David commanded his son, Solomon before his *bar mitzvah* "וְחָזַקְתָּ וְהָיִיתָ לְאִישׁ", *and you will be strong and you will become a man" (I Kings 2:2)*. The explanation of a *man* is one who fears sin because of his obligation to follow God's commandments (*Targum Yonasan*).

Rav Elazar said: Until thirteen years, man struggles with the physical component of his soul; after that time if he wishes to be a righteous person he will be given a spiritually elevated soul drawn from beneath the throne of the Heavenly King. (*Zohar Chadash, Genesis*).

Zohar about Bar Mitzvah

ـ§ A person begins to purify himself when he becomes thirteen years old (*Zohar, Vayishlach*).

ـ§ God deals kindly with the children of Israel, for when one reaches thirteen, He designates two angels to guard him along his path in life (*Zohar, Genesis* 165b).

ـ§ The fruits of a tree, during its first three years are considered *orlah*, i.e. they are forbidden to be eaten. Similarly, the first thirteen years of a boy's life are considered *orlah*, spiritually underdeveloped. After that time his soul is aroused to pursue spiritually elevated service to God, to prevent his physical drives from overtaking him (*Zohar Chadash, Genesis* 14a).

---

1. A question often raised, however, is how one can overcome his Evil Inclination if he is born with it, while his Good Inclination does not join him until he is thirteen?

The *Zohar* in *Vayeishev* comments that if God had not first instilled a *yetzer hora* in man when he is born, and he would have been created with a *yetzer tov* at birth, he would have had no free will. The presence of a *yetzer tov* would be too powerful an influence to ignore God's challenge to man to overcome his base desires.

The *Midrash Tanchuma (Genesis 7)* comments that man is the cause of his own *yetzer hara*. When a child is young he does not sin, and only as he grows older does he begin to succumb to his desires. God wishes to reward man for suppressing the tendencies which he has brought upon himself (*Tefillah l'Moshe*, introduction).

INSIGHTS AND ALLUSIONS

The verse in *Isaiah* (43:21) says: "עַם זוּ יָצַרְתִּי לִי תְּהִלָּתִי יְסַפֵּרוּ, *this is my nation which I have formed for me, they will speak of My praise.*"

Interpretations and References The age at which a boy becomes part of the nation of God, worthy to sing His praises in prayer is זוּ, which has the numerical equivalent of 13 (*Midrash Shmuel, Avos* 5:25).

⤐ The commentators question the use of the term *bar mitzvah* (literally: the son of a *mitzvah*), which connotes a filial relationship in regard to the performance of *mitzvos*. One who pursues a life of sin, however, is called a *ba'al aveirah*, literally: a husband, or master of sin. The difference can be explained as follows: The connection one has to commandments is eternal, just as the bond between father and son is never severed. The affinity one has to sin, however, is temporary; just as in a marriage or a proprietary relationship, the relationship can, if necessary, be terminated (*Hilchos V'Halichos Bar Mitzvah*).

⤐ The term used for one who reaches adulthood is *bar mitzvah*, rather than *ben mitzvah*. While both refer to one's acceptance of *mitzvos*, the former expression is Aramaic; the latter is Hebrew. *Bar* in Aramaic also means "outside of." Initially, when the child begins his life as a adult, he has not totally integrated the *mitzvos*, and they are external to him. Once he pursues them in earnest he becomes a *ben mitzvah* (*Meshech Chachmah*. See also Overview page 23).

⤐ "וַיְהִי עֶרֶב וַיְהִי בֹקֶר יוֹם אֶחָד, *and it was evening and it was morning one day*" (*Genesis* 1:5). When a child is born, he possesses an Evil Inclination, represented by the dark of night. The morning, which banishes darkness symbolizes the Good Inclination. The *one day* cited in the verse can refer to the day one becomes a *bar mitzvah*, since the numerical equivalent of אֶחָד is *13*. On this day the Good Inclination first appears to vanquish his evil counterpart (*Hegyonos Yitzchak*).

⤐ Just as the first three years of a fruit tree are considered *"orlah,"* and one is prohibited from eating its fruit, so too with man. Man, whom the Torah compares to a *tree of the field* (*Deuteronomy* 20:19), is closed off from Torah during the first three years of his life because his speech and understanding are not yet developed. After three years God gives him a ten-year period, in which he is

The First Mishnah
Rabbeinu Hakodesh started the first Mishnah in Shas with the topic of the recital of the Shema at night, for that is the first mitzvah commanded to a young man as he enters the age of mitzvos on the evening of his thirteenth birthday.
— Chiddushei HaRim, Berachos

infused with Torah. This period corresponds to the ten commandments heard at Mount Sinai. At that point he enters the age of manhood, obligated in the *mitzvos* and liable for their transgressions (*Rabbeinu Bachya, Avos*).

"הָלַךְ יֵלֵךְ וּבָכֹה נֹשֵׂא מֶשֶׁךְ הַזָּרַע בֹּא יָבֹא בְרִנָּה נֹשֵׂא אֲלֻמֹתָיו", *He who bears the measure of seeds walks along weeping, but will return in exultation, a bearer of his sheaves*" (*Psalms* 126:6).

The father, while his son is still young, is saddened, because he bears responsibility for the trangressions of his progeny. When he comes to the age of thirteen, however (יָבֹא numerically is *13*), then the father exults, as thereafter the child is responsible for his own actions. (R' Aharon of Belz at his own *bar mitzvah*).

אוֹר לְאַרְבָּעָה עָשָׂר בּוֹדְקִין אֶת הֶחָמֵץ לְאוֹר הַנֵּר, *On the eve of the fourteenth (of Nissan) we search for leaven by the light of the candle* (*Pesachim* 2a). The kabbalists make reference to the fact that on the eve of the fourteenth year of one's life, when one becomes *bar mitzvah*, one must search for leaven, represented by the Evil Inclination. The search takes place by the light of the candle, which represents Torah and its commandments. In this way man can seek out and destroy his Evil Inclination (*Arizal, Likutei Torah, Exodus*).

According to Scriptural law, if leaven is nullified in one's heart, i.e. mentally, it is sufficient for it to be considered void. Since, however, the Evil Inclination has been so much a part of the child for his first thirteen years of life, a thorough search must be made to ferret out the Evil Inclination from all the cracks and crevices where it may be hiding (*Toldos Yaakov Yosef*).

In the days of the four kings who battled the five kings (*Genesis* 14:1), the land was controlled by Chedorlaomer for thirteen years. In the fourteenth year the kings rose up in revolt and defeated him (*Genesis* 14:5). The life of a young man follows a similar pattern. During the first thirteen years of one's life, he is subjugated by his evil inclination since he has not permeated his life with Torah. From the time he enters his fourteenth year it is his responsibility to do battle with his evil inclination (*Aisan Ha'ezrachi* in *N'ki Chapayim*).

Additionally, becoming thirteen years old is significant relative to forty years of age. At that time our Sages say, "At forty, one

acquires understanding" (*Avos* 5:25). Just as wheat grain is only suitable for planting once it is one-third developed, so, too, once the young man has reached one-third of the age of understanding, at thirteen, he becomes suitable to plant the seeds of Torah, which he will ultimately develop (R' Pinchas of Koritz, *Hilchos v'Halichos Bar Mitzvah*, p. 225).

⋘ The symbolism of thirteen is discussed in light of it being a propitious age at which to acquire the three foundations of life mentioned in *Pirkei Avos*: Torah, service to God, and acts of loving kindness. Torah is elucidated through the use of thirteen principles. The child, upon receiving a circumcision, is compared to a sacrifice to God, consecrating him to a life of service. The Talmud (*Nedarim* 31b) comments that thirteen covenants were established concerning circumcision, as the word מִילָה is mentioned or alluded to thirteen times in *Genesis* 17. A new covenant with God is established on the day one becomes a *bar mitzvah*. This new covenant reinforces the inherent responsibility he accepted when he was but eight days old. The principle of loving kindness, *gemilas chasadim*, parallels the thirteen Attributes of Mercy possessed by God. (See page 47 for the complete listing). Now that the child has reached the age of responsibility, he can emulate the kindness bestowed upon him by God (*Ollelos Ephraim*).

⋘ When (King) David entered his fourteenth year, Scripture attributes the following to him: "ה׳ אָמַר אֵלַי בְּנִי אַתָּה אֲנִי הַיּוֹם יְלִדְתִּיךָ, *God said to me You are my son, I have begotten you this day*" (*Psalms* 2:7). Until that time David was not considered a *son of God*, as he had not merited a spiritually elevated soul. Until that time he was in the years of *orlah*, a state of spiritual under-development (*Zohar Mishpatim* 88:1).

⋘ The Number Thirteen — Its Significance

While the primary association of the number thirteen is with the age of *mitzvos*, we find many more references to that number throughout the Talmud and *Midrash*. Cited below are some of the references to the number thirteen.

The Thirteen *Midos* of Rabbi Yisrael Salanter

Rabbi Yisrael Lipkin of Salant (1809-1883) was the founder of the Mussar Movement, which developed teachings to help improve one's character through introspection and Torah study. The thirteen midos, cardinal principles, attributed to Reb Yisrael are a fitting creed for the young man or woman as he or she enters adulthood. Reb Yisrael encouraged his students to keep a diary listing these thirteen midos. By recording incidents in which these traits played a role, one could contemplate his mastery of them until he perfected them all.

Thirteen Attributes of Mercy

The Talmud (*Rosh Hashanah* 17b) relates that God wrapped Himself, as it were, like a *chazzan*, and showed Moses the Thirteen Attributes. 1. Hashem, 2. Hashem, 3. God, 4. Compassionate, 5. and Gracious, 6. Slow to anger, 7. Abundant in Kindness, 8. and Truth, 9. Preserver of kindness for thousands of generations, 10. Forgiver of iniquity, 11. Forgiver of willful sin, 12. and Forgiver of error, 13. and Who cleanses. He told Moses, "When the people of Israel sin, have them perform this order (of prayer) and they will be forgiven. This formulation, said in our *selichos* as well as our *Ne'ilah* prayer on *Yom Kippur*, outlines thirteen different expressions of compassion and forgiveness which reflect God's dealings with man (*Rosh Hashanah* 17b).

Thirteen Rules for Elucidating the Torah

These rules, or hermeneutic principles, refer to basic methods used in expounding the Torah as determined by oral tradition. These rules are listed in a formulation by Rabbi Yishmael, which concludes the section of the *Shacharis* service dealing with sacrificial offerings.

Thirteen Principles of Faith

These thirteen cardinal beliefs, based on the formulation of Maimonides, are recommended to be recited every day after *Shacharis*. They are grouped into three categories: the nature of belief in God, the authenticity of the Torah, and man's responsibility and ultimate reward.

Thirteen Covenants

The importance of circumcision is underscored by the fact that the Torah, in its introduction to the *mitzvah* (*Genesis* 17), refers to it thirteen times as a *bris*, a convenant (*Nedarim* 31b).

Thirteen Principles of Reb Yisrael Salanter

A list of thirteen virtues, attributed to Reb Yisrael Salanter, the founder of the Mussar Movement, outlines guidelines for life. These thirteen traits are essential for positive character development. They are shown in the art plate, previous page).

Thirteen Knots and Strings of *Tzitzis*

The Torah commandment to look at the *tzitzis* on one's garments and remember the commandments of God is alluded to

in the word צִיצִית itself. The numerical equivalent of צִיצִית is 600. The sum of the five knots and the eight strings of the *tzitzis* total thirteen. If one looks at the *tzitzis* with the proper intent it will help him remember the need to fulfill all 613 commandments (*Rashi, Numbers* 15:3).

◦§ Thirteen Expressions of Praise

The *Zohar* (*Terumah* 132a) refers to thirteen expressions of praise to God for His greatness and dominion. These thirteen are said in the יִשְׁתַּבַּח prayer, beginning with שִׁיר וּשְׁבָחָה. (The *Zohar* does not count the last two praises בְּרָכוֹת וְהוֹדָאוֹת, *blessings and thanksgivings*.)

◦§ The Patriarchs and Matriarchs

In the Hebrew names of the Patriarchs, אַבְרָהָם, יִצְחָק, יַעֲקֹב there are thirteen letters: In the Hebrew letters of the Matriarchs, שָׂרָה, רִבְקָה, רָחֵל, לֵאָה there are also thirteen letters.

◦§ The First Thirteen Years of Abraham's Life

The Midrash says: After Abraham was born, the king's officers wished to kill him, since his belief in a single God was contrary to the thinking of Nimrod and most others at that time. Consequently, he was forced to hide underground, where he lived for thirteen years. After this time he emerged, began speaking in the holy tongue (Hebrew) and despised idols and idol worship (*Pirkei d'Rav Eliezer*, chap. 26).

◦§ The Thirteen Children of Jacob

In addition to his twelve sons, Jacob also had one daughter, Dina. His family consisted of thirteen children.

◦§ The Thirteen Names of God

The Name of God is mentioned thirteen times in the narrative describing the first fruit offerings (*Deuteromomy* 26:1-10). These correspond to the Thirteen Attributes of Mercy (*Meshech Chachmah, Ki Savo*).

◦§ The Omer

There is a *halachah l'Moshe miSinai*, an oral tradition given to Moses at Mount Sinai, that in order to sift the flour for the *omer* very finely, it had to be sifted through thirteen different sieves. (*Menachos* 76b, *Rashi*, *loc.cit.*).

The Thirteen Years of Rabbi Shimon bar Yochai

Once Rabbi Yehudah, Rabbi Yose and Rabbi Shimon bar Yochai were sitting and discussing the seeming beneficence of the Romans for constructing marketplaces, bridges and bathhouses. Rabbi Yehudah praised their efforts, Rabbi Yose remained silent during the discussion, and Rabbi Shimon bar Yochai denounced them as being motivated by selfish gratification. Yehudah ben Gairim, who was present during the discussion, related the conversations to the Roman government. Rabbi Shimon and his son Rabbi Elazar fled to a cave where they were miraculously sustained by a carob tree and a spring of water.

For twelve years they studied Torah together until Elijah the Prophet stood at the entrance of the cave and informed them that the emperor had died. Rabbi Shimon, who had elevated himself to a level of holiness during those twelve years, was not accustomed to seeing people engage in mundane pursuits rather than the study of Torah. When he cast his holy eyes upon people involved in planting and harvesting, his mere glance caused destruction and desolation. A voice emanated from heaven, "Have you come out to destroy my world?" Rabbi Shimon and his son had to return to the cave for an additional twelve months. Only after Rabbi Shimon had remained in the cave for a full thirteen years was he able to reconcile his own spiritual elevation with the earthly existence of his fellow man (*Shabbos* 33b).

Thirteen Utensils in the Bais HaMikdash

The Mishnah (*Shekalim* 6:3) enumerates various items in the Holy Temple, each with the number thirteen. There were thirteen receptacles formed in the shape of a *shofar*, to collect coins for communal sacrifices. There were thirteen tables, or stands in the Holy Temple, used to rinse off the innards of the sacrifices and to hold the limbs until they were brought on the Altar. In the Holy Temple, the people bowed opposite the thirteen gates, as an expression of praise for the Temple's beauty. The Mishnah (*Midos* 2:3) also reports that the thirteen prostrations corresponded to thirteen breaches made by the Greeks in the Temple walls. When the Hashmonean kings repaired these breaches, the Sages decreed that one should bow opposite them as an expression of thanks.

INSIGHTS AND ALLUSIONS

The Thirteen Changes in the Septuagint

During the Second Temple era, King Ptolemy of Egypt gathered seventy Sages into different rooms to translate the Torah into Greek. He placed each sage in a separate room to ensure that they would not collude with one another, and to assure himself of the authenticity of the translation. They concluded their work on the eighth day of Teves. Miraculously, each of the Sages made the same thirteen changes in translation from the authentic version of the text to make it acceptable to Ptolemy (*Tractate Sofrim,* chap. 1). Despite the miraculous occurence, it was a day of sadness for the Jews because the Torah became accessible to the nations of the world, and its holy, exalted status became compromised (*Megillas Taanis*).

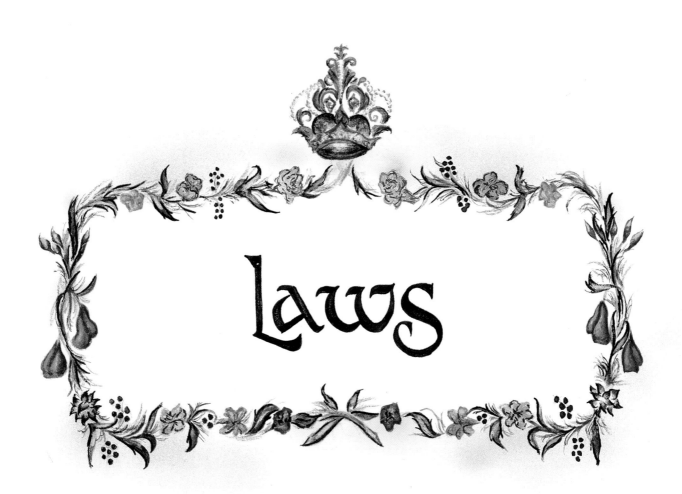

Laws

Laws and Responsa

By means of thorough research, keen analysis and brilliance of mind, our poskim, decisors, have grappled with halachic issues through the ages. Rabbi Akiva Eiger, one of the foremost halachic authorities of past generations tackled complex problems to clarify the truth implicit in the Torah. The issue of a child who ate a meal as a minor and became a gadol, a halachic adult, during the period of digestion is discussed here in light of his obligation in Grace after Meals.

קטן חייב מדרבנן מסתפקנא בכל יום
האחרון של שנת י"ד

לעת ערב קודש לילה ובתחלת הלילה
שנעשה גדול עדיין לא נתעכל המזון אס מחויב מדאו'
לברך. ואס נדין ד   א דאורייתא י"ל דאס צריך קודש
הלילה. דכשהו   צריך לחזור ולצרך כיון דצעידן
דצריך לא היה ח   "ת לצרך א"י לפטור היוצא
של דאורייתא. ע' מג   יס" סק"א ד"ה ול"ע עיי"ש.

אח"כ הראה לי ח   ד מהו' שמואל י"י דכעין
זה נסתפק ב   חכמת אדס דאס אכל
כשהוא חונן ונקצר המת   ז שנתעכל המזון אס
לריך לצרך. ויס לחלק ד   ת נמשך מהתחלת
האכילה עד אחר עיכ   א דצעידן דעוסק
במלוה. היינו בענינות פט   לצרך . בזה י"ל
דתיכף כשגמר המלוה ל   לעשות מלותו
דצרכת ר   ה נ"ד דעידן אזל   חיוצא . י"ל
ול"ע לדינא.   יו

Yonah Weinitz

Date Determination

 Jewish male becomes obligated to observe all the *mitzvos* at the first moment of the first day of the fourteenth year of his life. On this day he becomes a *bar mitzvah*.

A child's official (halachic) birthdate (which is also his *bar mitzvah* date) is determined according to the Hebrew calendar.

The exact time of birth is significant since each new Hebrew day actually commences at the beginning of the previous night. The date of birth which appears on a child's birth certificate may, therefore, not correspond to the correct Hebrew birthdate. If the child is born after nightfall, his Hebrew birth date is the one which corresponds to the following day.

If a child is born between sunset and the emergence of night (*bain hashmashos*), a competent halachic authority must be consulted in **Twilight Birth** order to correctly determine his true *bar mitzvah* date.

Sometimes a child's birth date and his *bar mitzvah* date are not the same. Such a situation could occur if the child is born on the 30th day **Birth in Cheshvan or Kislev** of the month of *Cheshvan* or *Kislev*, since those dates may simply not exist in the year of his *bar mitzvah*. This is because the number of days in these months is inconsistent from year to year. *Cheshvan* and *Kislev* can have 29 days in one year, while in other years one or both can have 30 days.

Note: Throughout this book *Orach Chaim* is abbreviated as O.C. and *Mishnah Berurah* as M.B.

A child born on the 30th day of *Cheshvan*, therefore, becomes a *bar mitzvah* on the first day of *Kislev*, if *Cheshvan* has only 29 days that year (*M.B.* 55:43).

Similarly, if a child is born on the first day of *Kislev* in a year when *Cheshvan* has 29 days, he would become a *bar mitzvah* on the 30th day of *Cheshvan*, in the event *Cheshvan* has 30 days in that year (*ibid.*).

The occurence of a leap year during the year of birth or *bar mitzvah* can complicate the *bar mitzvah* date determination process.

Adar Births and Rosh Chodesh Births

☐ A child born on Rosh Chodesh *Nissan* is not affected in any way by intercalation (the insertion of a second month of *Adar*). Even if the birth year contained 12 months and the *bar mitzvah* year 13 months, the child does not become a *bar mitzvah* until Rosh Chodesh *Nissan (ibid.)*.

☐ A child born during the first *Adar* of a leap year becomes a *bar mitzvah* within the first *Adar* of a leap year, according to most halachic authorities (*M.B.* 55:43; see also *Chasam Sofer*, *O.C.* chap. 14).

☐ A child born during *Adar* of a regular year becomes a *bar mitzvah* in the second *Adar* of a leap year (*Rama*, *O.C.* 55:10).

☐ A child born in the second *Adar*, will, of course, become a *bar mitzvah* in the second *Adar*, should that year also be a leap year (*M.B. loc. cit.*).

☐ A child born in either *Adar* of a leap year becomes a *bar mitzvah* in the only *Adar* of a non-leap year. Given this ruling it is possible for a younger child (born in the second *Adar*) to become a *bar mitzvah* before an older child (born in the first *Adar* of that same year), should their *bar mitzvah* not occur during a leap year (*O.C.* 55:10)!

This scenario is even conceivable with twins, if one was born on the 29th day of the first *Adar*, and his brother was born on the first day of the second *Adar*. The younger brother actually becomes a *bar mitzvah* 28 days before his older brother.

There is a dispute among authorities regarding the *bar mitzvah* date of a child born on the first day of Rosh Chodesh *Adar* of a regular year. Since that date is also the 30th day of *Shevat*, his *bar mitzvah* date during a leap year could either be the first day of Rosh Chodesh of the first *Adar* (30 *Shevat*), or the first day of Rosh Chodesh of the second *Adar* (the "real" *Adar*). A halachic authority should be consulted.

In addition to the requirement of completing thirteen full years of life, a boy does not attain the status of a *gadol,* halachic adult, until he

Puberty

reaches puberty. In halachic terms, puberty is defined as the stage in which two pubic hairs become discernible (*O.C.* 55:9).

Empirical observation of the pubic hairs is, however, not necessary before a boy is considered to be *bar mitzvah*. It is assumed that all boys over thirteen years old have also reached puberty. Even if an actual inspection does not reveal signs of pubescence, we may assume that the hairs were present, but subsequently fell off (*Rama, O.C.* 55:5).

With relation to fulfillment of *mitzvos* which are דְּאוֹרַיְיתָא, *of Scriptural origin*, however, it is questionable whether one should rely on a boy who has reached the age of *bar mitzvah* chronologically, but has not shown definitive evidence of having reached puberty. Such a boy should not recite *kiddush* on the Sabbath for the sake of adults who wish to fulfill this *mitzvah* by listening to him (*M.B.* 271:2). A halachic authority should be consulted.

A boy is considered to be a *bar mitzvah* by virtue of his father's testimony to that fact. That is, a boy can be counted in a *minyan* and

Determination Without Proof

may read from the Torah if his father says he is a *bar mitzvah,* even without any other confirmation (*M.B.* 55:41).

If no evidence is available regarding a boy's birth date, and his father does not know it or is not alive, an inquiry should be made of a halachic authority.

The mere declaration of a child regarding his birth date is not considered sufficient proof to determine his *bar mitzvah* date regarding accompanying obligations and privileges. (See *Tzafnas Pa'aneiach Nedarim,* chap. 11:3).

Generally, if a child is in a different time zone at the time of his *bar mitzvah* from the one in which he was born, his *bar mitzvah* date

Time Zones

remains unchanged.

If the International Date Line has been crossed, a consultation with a halachic authority is indicated.

Halachic literature is replete with scores of questions and responsa related to issues of *bar mitzvah* status and their ramifications. Many of the queries and their respective halachic decisions have applications which are relevant to daily and situational practice.

While it is rare that any full consensus of opinion actually emerges regarding most of these intricate dilemmas, a glimpse into the types of questions that could arise is in order.

The reader is cautioned not to utilize this section in any definitive halachic fashion. Rather, it is hoped that the issues discussed here will be used as a springboard to raise one's consciousness about the scope of questions which can arise. As always, a competent Rabbinic authority should be consulted. . . .

The sampling of halachic responsa presented here is by no means exhaustive. Indeed, the range of potential questions is immense. What follows is a selection of some of the more common categories of halachic problems, examples within each category, and a few of the respected opinions on the suggested rulings to follow in those cases.

Actions Performed by a Minor

There are several actions that the halachah requires be done only by someone who is a *bar mitzvah*.

ᥑ *Sefer Torah*

The writing of a *Sefer Torah* (Torah scroll), *tefillin*, or a *mezuzah* must be done by a *gadol* (someone over *bar mitzvah* age). These items, if written by a minor, are considered *posul*, invalid (*O.C.* 39:1). This law applies even to a *kesher*, knot of the *tefillin*, which was tied by a minor. Such a knot should be undone and tied again by a *gadol* (*Be'ur Halachah O.C.* 39:2).

ᥑ *Mezuzah*

If a minor affixes a *mezuzah* to a doorpost, a question arises whether the *mezuzah* should be removed and reattached and if so, whether a *brachah* should then be recited (see *Pischei Teshuvah*, *Y.D.* 291, note 4; also *Nachlas Zvi*, *Y.D. ibid*; *Yabbia Omer*, Part III, *O.C.* 27, note 9).

◆§ *Succos*

It is considered preferable for a *succah* to be built and covered by someone who is a *bar mitzvah* (*Bikurei Yaakov* 635). Similarly, a *gadol* should bind the species to the *lulav* for *Succos* (*M.B.* 649:14 and *Shaarei Tzion, ibid.*). If undoing the minor's binding and re-tying it, is not possible, it can still be used as is.

◆§ Ritual Slaughter

A similar question arises when a minor slaughters an animal. Unless an adult is supervising the procedure, a minor is not permitted to slaughter an animal (see *Rama* and *Shach, Y.D.* 5:5). As to whether the minor himself may be permitted to eat from this animal, see *Darkei Teshuvah* chap. 28 note 127.

Obligations Fulfilled Retroactively By a Minor

This category deals with situations when a minor, who performs a *mitzvah*, then becomes a *gadol*. In question is whether his fulfillment of the obligations carries over sufficiently to exempt him from repeating the *mitzvah* once he has become a *bar mitzvah*.

◆§ *Bircas HaTorah*

For example, *halachah* requires that every morning we say the *bircas haTorah*, blessings prior to learning Torah (*O.C.* 471,2 and *M.B. ibid.*). The question arises if a minor's recital of these blessings in the morning allows him to learn Torah later that evening, when he first becomes a *gadol*. Is it necessary for him to repeat these blessings at night, prior to his learning, since he is now a *bar mitzvah?*

Many authorities do not obligate the boy to repeat the *bircas haTorah* at night (see *Maharsham* — Vol. III, chap. 121). Others are of the opinion that a blessing recited as a minor might not be valid later — when he becomes a *gadol (Yabbia Omer* Vol. III, chap. 27).

An interesting solution to this dilemma might be to advise the youngster, before he davens *Maariv*, to have in mind when he recites the *Ahavas Olam* blessing, that he is fulfilling the obligation of *bircas haTorah* with that part of *Maariv* (see *Yabbia Omer, ibid.*).

The *Ahavas Olam* blessing of *Maariv*, just as in *Shacharis*, is valid for fulfilling the *bircas haTorah* obligation (*M.B.* 47:13).

Kiddush Levanah

If a youngster has a choice of performing a *mitzvah* before or after his *bar mitzvah*, it is advisable for him to wait until he is a *gadol*. The *mitzvah* of *kiddush levanah*, blessing of the new moon, is a good example of this. If sufficient time allows for the blessing to be made when he is a *gadol*, then some say it is better to wait until then. If he recites the blessing while he is still a minor he has fulfilled his obligation and need not repeat the *mitzvah* (*Yabbia Omer* Vol. III, chap. 27).

Maariv

The evening service, *Maariv*, can be recited before nightfall actually arrives (*O.C.* 235:1). It is, however, not recommended for a minor, who will become a *bar mitzvah* when the *Sabbath* begins, to be the *shliach tzibbur*, congregation leader, if *Maariv* is said before nightfall. This is because the lad had not actually completed a full thirteen years of life by nightfall (*Rama, O.C. 53:10* and *M.B. op.cit.* note 33).

Kiddush

A boy who will become a *bar mitzvah* on the *Sabbath* or on a Festival should not recite *kiddush* until nightfall has actually arrived. Prior to that, he is still considered a minor (*Ben Ish Chai* Vol. III, *Genesis,* note 14; also *Imrei Binah, Hilchos Shabbos,* chap. 11 and *Binyan Shlomo,* chap. 60). Some rule that the *kiddush*, if recited early, must be repeated (*Imrei Binah ibid.* and *Binyan Shlomo ibid.*). Others do not require this. Should this question arise, it is best to listen to *kiddush* again from someone else (*Yabbia Omer*, Vol. III, chap. 27-28).

Shehechiyanu

Should a boy who becomes a *bar mitzvah* during a Festival, i.e. *Passover* or *Succos*, repeat the *shehechiyanu* blessing after he becomes a *gadol?*

Since no consensus of opinion exists regarding this matter, it might be preferable for the boy to find some special reason to say the *shehechiyanu* blessing. The recitation of this *brachah* for a new fruit or significant article of clothing will exempt him from saying the *brachah* again for the Festival.

Chanukah

A boy who reaches *bar mitzvah* status during Chanukah should be aware of the clock. While he might ordinarily kindle the

Chanukah lights 15 minutes before nightfall (*M.B.* chap. 672, note 1), on the night of his *bar mitzvah* he should wait until actual nightfall.

◆§ Mourning

Considerable dispute exists regarding the practice that a boy should follow, if God forbid, he is in a seven-day or thirty-day mourning period when he becomes a *bar mitzvah*.

Some rule that the mourning periods for him begin on the day of his *bar mitzvah* (*Maharam M'Rotenberg* cited by *Rosh, Moed Katan* chap. 3, Part 96; also *Bach* on *Tur, Yoreh Deah*, chap. 396).

The prevailing opinion, however, is that mourning periods are dictated only from the first moment of the relative's death. Since at that time he was a minor, no mourning period at all is observed (*Shulchan Aruch*, Y.D. 396:3 and *Taz* note 2); *Chachmas Adam* 168:6; *Aruch HaShulchan*, Y.D. *loc. cit*, note 8).

Still others are of the minority opinion that the remaining days of *shivah*, seven days of mourning and *shloshim,* thirty-day mourning period, should be observed if there are other adult mourners (*Tiferes L'Moshe* on *Yoreh Deah loc.cit*. See also *P'sakim V'takanos Rabbi Akiva Eiger*, chap. 3). Even if other adults are not mourning, the remaining mourning period should be observed, according to some (Rabbi Akiva Eiger, *ibid.*).

Mitzvos Caused by Actions of Minors

This category deals with those *mitzvos* which *arrive* when someone is a *gadol*, but are caused by actions that he performed while still a minor.

◆§ *Bircas HaMazon*

A classic example of such a case is the question of *bircas hamazon*, grace after meals. If a boy ate a meal while he was still a minor, but finished his meal after nightfall — and is now a *bar mitzvah* — is he required by the Torah to *bentch*, say grace? (Of course, even a minor should *bentch* because of the Rabbinical obligation of *chinuch*. Here the question is whether a Torah obligation exists).

A related question is whether he must repeat the *bircas hamazon* at night if he said it before nightfall. Those who would

הלכות
laws
ותשובות

require the repetition of *bircas hamazon* after nightfall, reason that the Torah obligates one to *bentch* when he is *satisfied* after eating. As it is written: "‏וְאָכַלְתָּ וְשָׂבָעְתָּ וּבֵרַכְתָּ...‏", (*Deuteronomy* 8:10). That satisfaction is present after he becomes a *bar mitzvah* and the requirement lasts until the food is digested, approximately seventy-two minutes (*O.C.* 184:5). Perhaps he must now fulfill his Torah obligation, even though he said the *bircas hamazon* a short time earlier — when he was a minor.

Others disagree, believing that the eating is what caused the obligation to *bentch*. Since the eating took place when he was a minor — the *bircas hamazon* that he recited when he was a minor is sufficient (*Hagaos Rabbi Akiva Eiger, O.C.* 186:2; *K'sav Sofer O.C.* 31; *Imrei Binah O.C.* 15; *Chazon Ish, O.C.* 25).

If he had *not* said the *bircas hamazon* before nightfall it is questionable whether his obligation to *bentch* is now Scriptural or Rabbinic (*ibid.*). Because of this doubt, he should not lead the *bircas hamazon* for a group of three or ten, (*Kaf Hachaim* 199, note 32), nor should he say the *bircas hamazon* out loud to exempt others. It is even questionable whether he can be included in a group of three or ten who have a Scriptural requirement to *bentch* (see *Rama, O.C.* 199:10).[1]

Mitzvos That Begin When One is a Minor and Continue After He is Thirteen

There are certain *mitzvos* which can begin when one is a minor and continue while he is becoming a *gadol*. The halachic discussion centers on the question of whether the *gadol* has an obligation to fulfill this *mitzvah* — even though it began when he was still a minor — and, if so, what is the nature of this requirement — Scriptural or Rabbinic?

◆§ Sefiras Ha'Omer

The most common example of this type of dilemma is the *mitzvah* of *sefiras ha'omer*, the counting of the 49 days of the *omer*, from the second day of Passover until Shavuos.

The problem is particularly intriguing and intricate. While the

---

1. There is even one opinion that believes that there is neither a Scriptural nor Rabbinic requirement to *bentch* in that situation! The Scriptural obligation is not present because the eating took place when he was a minor. The Rabbinic requirement is also not there since he is no longer a minor at this time (The periodical *Shaarei Zion*, Num. VI, chap. 69.).

Torah instructs us to count each consecutive day of the *omer* in order for the entire *mitzvah* to be complete "תְּמִימוֹת,, there is a dispute regarding whether the counting of all 49 days constitutes the fulfillment of one *mitzvah* or whether the counting of each day represents a separate *mitzvah*. Our custom is to consider both opinions to be valid. Therefore, if someone misses one day of counting, he continues to count on the other days, but without a blessing.

Some authorities utilize the above distinction in their ruling. According to those who consider *sefiras ha'omer* one *mitzvah*, the boy does not recite a *brachah* when he becomes *bar mitzvah* during the *omer* because he had no Torah obligation when the *mitzvah* began — since he was a minor [*Avnei Nezer, O.C.* 539, and others). Counting the *omer* without a *brachah* is, of course, still required by all opinions.

According to those who view each day's counting as a separate *mitzvah*, the *gadol* should recite the *brachah* since his new obligatory status will now require him to perform the *mitzvah* each day.

Other authorities do not agree that the ruling is dependent on whether this is one *mitzvah* or forty-nine daily *mitzvos*. Some rule that even if the *omer* counting is one *mitzvah*, a boy, whose *bar mitzvah* date falls during the *omer*, should recite the *brachah* anyway (*Shaarei Teshuvah, O.C.* 489, note 20; *Aruch HaShulchan loc.cit.* note 25; *Teshuvos K'Sav Sofer, O.C.* 99 and others). Others rule that, conversely, even if the *omer* counting is a separate *mitzvah* each day — there is no obligation for a boy who becomes a *bar mitzvah* during *sefirah* to count the *omer* with a blessing (*Mo'adim U'zmanim*, chap. 288; *Minchas Elazar* vol. III, chap. 60).

Miscellaneous

The following are just a few of the miscellaneous issues that are dealt with in the *Responsa* literature, but do not fit into any of the previously mentioned categories.

☐ Is it permissible or appropriate to allow a *bar mitzvah* boy to be called to the Torah, have an *aliyah*, if his mother, who is Jewish, is still married to the boy's gentile father? (See *Igros Moshe, O.C.* vol. II, chap. 73).

הלכות
Laws
ותשובות

☐ Can a *bar mitzvah* boy who is not circumcised receive an *aliyah*? (See *Seridei Aish* vol. II, chap. 10; *Tzitz Eliezer* vol. XI, chap. 9).

☐ Is it permissible for a person, during his one year mourning period, to attend the festive *bar mitzvah* meal if the boy will deliver his *drashah*, sermon, during the meal? (See *Dagul Me'revavah, Y.D.* 391:2; also *Teshuvos Tuv Ta'am Vodaas*, Vol. III, chap. 86).

☐ Does a gentile have the status of a minor or a *gadol*, and what criteria are used to determine his status? This question is relevant when choosing a gentile to purchase one's *chametz*, leaven, prior to Passover (*Teshuvos Chasam Sofer, Y.D.* chap. 317). (See also *Mishnah Torah, Rambam, Hilchos Melachim* 10:2).

Gift Giving

Caution must sometimes be exercised when giving gifts to the *bar mitzvah* boy. This is because of the prohibition of giving a gift on the Sabbath or on a Festival unless it is for the purpose of the Sabbath or for a *mitzvah* (*M.B.* 306:33).

It is, therefore, advisable *not* to give the present to a *bar mitzvah* boy on the Sabbath or on a Festival. If there is no practical alternative, the gift may be given provided that one of the following conditions is met:

1. Someone other than the *bar mitzvah* boy should acquire the gift for him at some time prior to the Sabbath (*Kappei Aharon*, Vol. I chap. 59).

2. The *bar mitzvah* boy himself receives the gift, but bears in mind not to take actual possession of it until after the Sabbath (*Shemiras Shabbos K'Hilchasa* p. 168).

Gifts . . . Why?
The custom of sending presents to the boy on his bar mitzvah day takes its roots from Purim. On Purim we rejoice and send gifts of food to one another, in celebration for the Jews renewing their commitment to Torah and accepting the mitzvos with free will and intention.
Similarly, we exult the inception of the boy into the bar mitzvah community and his acceptance of the yoke of mitzvos, by sending gifts to him on his bar mitzvah day.
— Aish Das

TEFILLIN

Donning the *Tefillin*

   The background is formed from the four parshiyos, the four Torah portions found in the tefillin. The picture is adapted from a postcard from Germany, circa 1906, courtesy of Holyland Treasures, Burlingame, California. From the hat pictured by the artist it seems that such was the custom of the bar mitzvah boy, a sign of maturity and "coming of age."

וידבר ידוה אל משה לאמר קדש לי כל ב
אתכם מזה ולא יאכל חמץ היום אתם יצאיו
הזאת בחדש הזה שבעת ימים תאכל מצת
לי בצאתי ממצרים והיה לך לאות על ידך

והיה כי ... יה אל ארש ... כאשר נ
וכל ה... פדה בשדה ... תפלה.
ידוה ... ת עבדי ... קשה.
פטר ה... כל בב...

יהיה אם שמע תשמעו אל מצותי א...
ונתתי עשב בשדך לבהמתך ואכלת ושב...
יבולה ואבדתם מהרה מעל הארץ הטבו.
בם בשבתך בביתך ובלכתך בדרך ובש...

TEFILLIN

תפילין

⋖§ Source and Significance

he commandment to wear *tefillin* is Biblical in origin. The Torah mandates: „וּקְשַׁרְתָּם לְאוֹת עַל יָדֶךְ וְהָיוּ לְטֹטָפֹת בֵּין עֵינֶיךָ", *"and you shall tie them as a sign on your hand and they shall be as tefillin between your eyes"* (Deuteronomy 6:8, 11:18).

The significance of the *mitzvah* of *tefillin* is great, in that the Torah mentions its requirement eight times. Consequently, the reward to its adherents is equally imposing. One who properly fulfills the *mitzvah* of *tefillin* lengthens his life on this world, as it says, „ה׳ עֲלֵיהֶם יִחְיוּ", *"those who carry the name of God on them will live (Isaiah 38:16; M.B. 37:1)."* A place in the World to Come is also assured to those who put on *tefillin*, wrap themselves with a *talis*, read the *Shema* and pray (*Tur* 37).

Conversely, those who do not fulfill this paramount *mitzvah*, even occasionally, because they do not adequately value the *mitzvah* of *tefillin*, are deemed to be in the category of „פּוֹשְׁעֵי יִשְׂרָאֵל בְּגוּפָן", *transgressors of Israel who sin with their bodies (O.C. 37:1).*

Meaning

The word „תְּפִילִּין", comes from the word פְּלִילָה. *Tur (O.C. 25),* therefore, connects *tefillin* to the concepts of testimony and proof (see also *Bach ibid*). Wearing *tefillin*, therefore, is seen as a declaration of proof that the *shechinah*, Divine Presence, rests upon the Jewish people. *Tefillin* worn on the head

---

Note: This section is not intended to constitute a comprehensive treatment of all the *halachos* of *tefillin*. It is merely a digest of the salient features of this essential *mitzvah*.

The reader is encouraged to study in fullest detail the *halachos* of *tefillin* as presented in the *Shulchan Aruch* and the *Mishnah Berurah*, and their commentaries. Specific questions of halachah should be directed to a competent halachic authority.

A Convincing Argument
R' Levi Yitzchak of Berditchev was often referred to as the "defense attorney" of the Jewish people. Never would he miss an opportunity to cast his brethren in a positive light.

In one of his frequent pleas to Hashem he was overheard saying:

"Ribbono Shel Olam!" You must forgive the iniquities of Your People. And if you do not, I will reveal the secret to the entire world that God wears tefillin that are posul, invalid, since the Talmud (Berachos 6a) relates that even Hashem wears tefillin. Inside the tefillin is written the phrase: „וּמִי כְּעַמְּךָ יִשְׂרָאֵל, גּוֹי אֶחָד בָּאָרֶץ" *"And who is like Your nation Israel, one People on this land."*

"But if, forbid it, You do not forgive their sins, he reasoned, "they will lose their exclusivity. If they cannot be called גּוֹי אֶחָד, one People — Your tefillin must be rendered invalid!"

TEFILLIN
תפילין

symbolizes this concept, since it contains the letters *shin* and *dalet* of the Holy Name שַׁדַּי.

Tefillin are referred to as an אות — *an eternal sign* of the everlasting unity of God. They are symbolic of the *Exodus* of the Jewish people from Egypt, by means of the miracles and wonders that He performed for us.

The designated areas of the body where *tefillin* are worn also point to the significance of this *mitzvah*. When putting *tefillin* on, we should have in mind that God has commanded us to bind these *tefillin* on the arm to recall the outstretched arm of the *Exodus*. It should be placed opposite the heart, thereby subjugating the desires and thoughts of our hearts to His service. *Tefillin* are also placed on the head opposite the brain, so that the soul therein, together with the other potentials, may all be subjugated to His service. His strength and dominion over those above and those below to do with them as He wishes, should also be mentally acknowledged.

◄§ *What are Tefillin?*

There are actually two distinct parts to the *mitzvah* of *tefillin* — the *tefillah shel yad* — which is worn on the arm, and the *tefillah shel*

Two Independent Mitzvos

rosh — which is worn on the head. (The word *tefillah* is the singular form of the word *tefillin*).

If someone has only one of the two *tefillin*, or if because of injury he cannot put on both, he should put one *tefillah* on. If he can choose the one to be worn, a question should be asked of a competent halachic authority as to which *tefillah* takes precedence. Such a rare circumstance might occur if he is traveling with a group which refuses to wait for him. If he will be able to put on the other *tefillah* later, he may put one of them on now. If not, then both must be put on right away (*M.B.* 26:1).

Parts of the Tefillin

Each *tefillah* consists of three basic parts: the *parshiyos*, the *batim*, and the *retzuos*.

☐ *Parshiyos*
Each *tefillah* contains within it four sections of the Torah. Each of

Shel Yad and *Shel Rosh* —
Why the Difference?
Both the tefillin shel yad and the tefillin shel rosh have four parshiyos written on parchment which are inserted into the batim. The parshiyos of the shel yad are all written on one parchment which is contained within one compartment. The parshiyos of the shel rosh, however, are written on four different parchments and are housed in four separate compartments. Why? R' Chaim of Volozhin explains that there are four senses in the head and each one is visible and separate — seeing, hearing, smelling and speaking. That is why the parshiyos of the shel rosh are separately written and housed.
The Talmud relates (Berachos 61a-b) that there are also four senses in the rest of the body — the heart understands, the kidneys give counsel, the spleen causes laughter and the hands can touch. These functions are not visible to the eye and all are contained within the body. The shel yad parshiyos are thus appropriately written and inserted. Each parshah has the potential to cleanse each bodily function.
— Nefesh Hachaim

these sections — all of which mention *tefillin* — must be handwritten by a scribe on parchment. They are:

קַדֶּשׁ לִי כָל בְּכוֹר (*Exodus* 13:1-10)

וְהָיָה כִּי יְבִיאֲךָ (*Exodus* 13:11-16)

שְׁמַע יִשְׂרָאֵל (*Deuteronomy* 6:4-9)

וְהָיָה אִם שָׁמעַ (*Deuteronomy* 11:13-21)

These four *parshiyos* are written on one strip of parchment in the *shel yad* and on four separate strips in the *shel rosh*

☐ *Batim*

Each *tefillah* has a casing into which the respective *parshiyos* are inserted. This casing is called a *bayis (batim*, in plural form).

The *batim* are made of leather which is produced from hides of kosher animals only and is specifically designated for this purpose — *lishmah*. Hides of oxen are considered to be the strongest and most durable of all kosher species. The entire *bayis* of the *shel yad* and the *shel rosh* should each be constructed from one piece of leather. This one piece of leather is then formed into four separate compartments to comprise the *shel rosh*. Each of the four *parshiyos* mentioned above is placed in its own compartment. Due to the complexity and precision prescribed by the laws concerning the proper construction of *batim*, one must exercise extreme diligence and discernment in selecting a skilled and reliable person from whom to purchase *batim*.

The *batim* must be perfectly square in length and width. This requirement applies not only to the *bayis* but also to the *titurah* and the *tefiros (O.C.* 32:39). The *titurah* is the base upon which the *bayis* rests. The *tefiros* are the stitches which close the *tefillah* and join the top and bottom of the *titurah*. The *bayis* of the *shel rosh* must have the letter *shin* protruding on the right and left sides. The *shin* on the right side of the wearer must be three-headed; the left side has four heads (*O.C.* 32:42). The *batim* should be painted black, with the paint coming from kosher materials (*O.C.* 32:37). It is especially important for the *shin* on each side of the *shel rosh* to always be purely black (*O.C.* 32:40). It cannot be overemphasized that whenever any doubt arises in regard to the status of the *kashrus* of the *tefillin*, a competent halachic authority must be consulted. These laws are particularly complex and only an expert who is fully acquainted with them can be relied upon.

Shin = 300*

One of the reasons why the letter "shin" is displayed on the outside of the tefillin is because it symbolizes the 300 days a year that one wears tefillin.

— Rabbeinu Bachya;
Parshas Ki Savo

These are the 65 days a year after tefillin are not worn: 52 days of Shabbos; 4 days of Pesach; 4 days of Succos; 2 days of Shavous; 2 days of Rosh Hashanah; 1 day of Yom Kippur = 65 days total.

*Shin has a numerical value of 300.

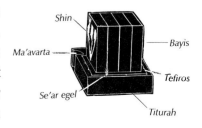

☐ *Retzuos* — Straps

The *retzuos* are the leather straps which are inserted through an opening in each of the *tefillin* which is called the *ma'avarta*. The *retzuos* are used to tighten the *tefillin* upon one's arm. The *retzuos*, like the *batim*, must be manufactured *lishmah* — for the express purpose of *tefillin*, and must be painted black *lishmah* as well. Only the outer side of the *retzuos*, however, needs to be painted. Halachically, the *retzuah* of the *shel yad* should be long enough to encircle the upper arm, be tied three times around the middle finger, and fastened. On a practical level, it should also be long enough to be wrapped seven times on the forearm (*O.C.* 27:8).

The *retzuos* of the *shel rosh* should extend at least to one's navel. It is customary that the right *retzuah* should reach the place of one's *milah*, circumcision, and the left *retzuah* should reach the navel. Others extend the right *retzuah* to the navel and the left to the chest (*O.C.* 27:11; *M.B.* 41). The minimum width of any *retzuah* is the length of a grain of barley. According to varying opinions this translates to a minimum width of nine or eleven millimeters. Should a tear, fold, or fray develop in a *retzuah* a halachical authority should be consulted.

◄§ *Kesharim*

The *retzuos* on both the *tefillin shel yad* and the *tefillin shel rosh* must form certain letter-shaped knots (*kesharim*). These knots must be formed *lishmah*, by an adult male.

The *kesher*, knot, on the *shel yad* is made to form the letter 'yud'; on the *shel rosh*, the letter 'dalet.' Some make a shape like a square box. Together with the 'shin' on the *bayis* of the *shel rosh*, the word "Sha-dai" (a name of God) is formed.[1]

One final requirement exists in the construction of the *tefillin shel rosh*, the *se'ar agel*, hair of a calf. Each *parshah* of the *shel rosh* is wrapped with a small piece of parchment and the hair of a calf. The ends of the hair used to wrap the *parshah* וְהָיָה אִם שָׁמֹעַ should extend out of its compartment and protrude out of the *titurah*, making it visible to all.

◄§ The *Sofer*

The *sofer*, scribe, must be an adult Jewish male who has acquired the physical signs deeming him halachically mature.

---

1. According to some the 'dalet' is formed by the two *retzuos* protruding from the *kesher* of the *shel rosh* (*Rashi, Shabbos* 62b).

Tears of Inspiration
When the great Rebbe R' Velvel of Zbarish, זצ"ל, was growing up there were no discernible signs that he was, in any way, more exceptional than any of his peers.

With his bar mitzvah date approaching, his father, R' Michel of Zlotshov, זצ"ל arranged for a prominent sofer in town to write and prepare tefillin for the lad. R' Michel invited the scribe to his home and requested that before the parshiyos would actually be inserted into the batim, the sofer should bring them to him.

Upon completion, the batim were brought to R' Michel. The Rebbe clutched them tightly in his hands, and then, with deepest concentration and heartfelt emotion he began to weep. The tears dropped softly into the batim and the crying didn't stop until the batim were full!

R' Michel then emptied the tears from the batim and ordered the parshiyos to be inserted only after the batim were dry.

On the day of his bar mitzvah, when R' Velvel first wore the tefillin, an extraordinary aura of kedushah descended upon him. From that day on, his great wisdom and outstanding leadership became renowned for generations to come.

Tefillin can be considered kosher only if the *sofer* who writes the *parshiyos* is a יְרֵא שָׁמַיִם, a *God-fearing person* who is fully knowledgeable in all the *halachos*, laws, of *tefillin*.

A determination of the *sofer's* piety and scholarship is essential since much trust must be placed in him. Mere empirical examination of the actual *k'sav*, lettering, of the *parshiyos* might only reveal the *sofer's* artistic capacities and meticulous attention to detail. Inspection of the finished product, however, does not provide testimony as to whether the writing and entire manufacturing process was actually done *lishmah* — for the specific purpose of making the *tefillin*. Indeed, the absence of *lishmah*, does, in many instances, render the *tefillin posul*, invalid.

The existence of correctly written *parshiyos* also does not prove that they were written *kesidran*, in order. It is necessary for the four *parshiyos* to be written in the correct sequence (see page 74) and for each letter of each word to be written in the order it appears in the Torah. Only the statement of the *sofer* himself can testify to his adherence to these criteria. The character and integrity of the *sofer* is, therefore, paramount when purchasing *tefillin*.

◆§ *Tefillin* of *Rashi* and *Rabbeinu Tam*

As stated previously, four *parshiyos* of the Torah are written on parchment and inserted into the *tefillin*. There is, however, a difference of opinion regarding the order in which these *parshiyos* appear in the *shel yad* and the placing of these *parshiyos* in the *shel rosh*.

According to *Rashi*, the order of the *parshiyos* in both *tefillin* is:

1) קָדֶשׁ 2) וְהָיָה כִּי יְבִיאֲךָ 3) שְׁמַע יִשְׂרָאֵל 4) וְהָיָה אִם שָׁמֹעַ

According to the view of *Rabbeinu Tam* the order is:

1) קָדֶשׁ 2) וְהָיָה כִּי יְבִיאֲךָ 3) וְהָיָה אִם שָׁמֹעַ 4) שְׁמַע יִשְׂרָאֵל

The first *parshah* is inserted into the first compartment to the left of the wearer.

Even according to *Rabbeinu Tam*, however, the *parshiyos* must actually be *written* according to the sequence they appear in the Torah (שְׁמַע prior to וְהָיָה אִם שָׁמֹעַ).

The halachah is in accordance with *Rashi's* view, but individuals who are especially exacting in their observance of *mitzvos*, also don the *tefillin* of *Rabbeinu Tam* after the *tefillin* of *Rashi* (without a *brachah*) and recite שְׁמַע and וְהָיָה אִם שָׁמֹעַ and other prayers while wearing them.

There is another distinction between *Rashi tefillin* and *Rabbeinu Tam tefillin*. Since the *se'ar agel*, hair of a calf, must protrude from the compartment of the *shel rosh* which contains וְהָיָה אִם שָׁמֹעַ, the hair will be visible in a different location depending on whether the *tefillin* are *Rashi* or *Rabbeinu Tam*. In *Rashi tefillin* the hair will extend out of the hole between the third and fourth compartment. In the *tefillin* of *Rabbeinu Tam*, the hair will stick out of the hole between the second and third compartments.

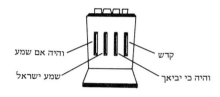

קדש — שמע ישראל
והיה כי יביאך — והיה אם שמע

The order of the parshiyos in the shel rosh (Rashi)

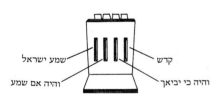

קדש — שמע ישראל
והיה כי יביאך — והיה אם שמע

The order of the parshiyos in the shel rosh (Rabbeinu Tam)

◆§ *Who is Required to Wear Tefillin?*

Every adult male is required by the Torah to wear *tefillin*. This obligation begins as soon as a boy becomes a *bar mitzvah* — at the age of thirteen years and one day. By that time, a father must have acquired *tefillin* for his son and have seen to it that he learns the *halachos* of *tefillin*.

Since *tefillin* is a מִצְוַת עֲשֵׂה שֶׁהַזְמַן גְּרָמָא, *a mitzvah which is dependent on a designated time*, i.e. *tefillin* are *not* worn on the Sabbath and Festivals, women are exempt from putting on *tefillin* (O.C. 38:3). Unlike the *mitzvos* of shofar and lulav, the *mitzvah* of *tefillin* should not be performed by women even if they desire to do so (*Rama ibid; see also Igros Moshe O.C. Vol. IV chap.* 49).

⊸§ *When to Begin*

Although the obligation for this *mitzvah* does not begin until *bar mitzvah* age, many have the custom to begin wearing *tefillin* from one to three months prior to *bar mitzvah*. This preparatory period is frequently established in order to familiarize the soon-to-be *bar mitzvah* boy with the laws, customs, and procedures of proper *tefillin* wear and care. Under no circumstances should a younger child put on *tefillin* for recreational purposes (see Customs section).

⊸§ *Exemption*

Maintenance of a clean body is a prerequisite for fulfillment of the *mitzvah* of *tefillin* (*O.C.* 38:1). Those who may not be able to maintain a clean body, because of a serious physiological condition, may be exempt from wearing *tefillin* during those times. Naturally, only a halachic authority can determine this. Similarly, one must also be diligent in keeping one's mind clean and free of distraction while wearing *tefillin* (*O.C.* 38:4). During the times that *tefillin* are worn, one must be constantly cognizant that he is wearing them. Consequently, if an ailment or stressful situation might potentially jeopardize his powers of concentration, he should ask a halachic authority to see if the situation warrants a temporary exemption.

A mourner, on the day of burial may be exempt from wearing *tefillin (O.C.* 38:5). Even if the burial had already taken place, hearing about a death may exempt the mourner from *tefillin* on that day — or at least from the *brachah*. A competent Rav should be consulted whenever questions arise regarding a mourner.

⊸§ *When are Tefillin Worn?*

The *mitzvah* of wearing *tefillin* requires one to wear them constantly — during day and night hours. However, because of other mitigating considerations, (see below), the current custom is to limit *tefillin* wear to the duration of *Shacharis*, the morning prayer. At the very least, one is required to wear *tefillin* during the recital of the *Shema* and *Shemoneh Esrei* (*O.C.* 25:4; *M.B.* 14).

Our Sages prohibited *tefillin* wear at night, lest one fall asleep while the *tefillin* are still on (*O.C.* 30:2). Moreover, since one must

constantly maintain a clean body while the *tefillin* are worn and be fully aware that he is wearing them, *tefillin* wear throughout the day is also not common practice. (Unlike our Sages, who, in the time of the Gemara *did* wear *tefillin* all day.)

If, because of some unforeseen circumstance, *tefillin* could not be obtained or worn at the time of *Shacharis*, one should recite his prayers, including *Shema* and *Shemoneh Esrei*, without them (*M.B.* 25:4). *Shema* should be repeated when the *tefillin* are worn later in the day (*M.B.* 58:5). If one is unable to put on *tefillin* until after sunset, he should still do so until nightfall (*M.B.* 30:3). This is true even if he already davened *Maariv*, evening prayers. A *brachah*, in that case, however, should not be recited (*Be'ur Halachah*, *O.C.* 30:5). It is most vital, that not even a single day pass without putting on *tefillin* (excluding, of course, the Sabbath and Festivals).

⋖ *Time of Day*

The earliest time of day that one may put on *tefillin* is from the moment that a person can recognize an acquaintance at a distance of six to eight feet (*O.C.* 30:1). This is usually about forty minutes before sunrise. In special situations when the *tefillin* can only be put on earlier, a Rabbinic authority should be consulted.

⋖ *Shabbos*

Wearing *tefillin* on the Sabbath and Festivals is forbidden. Since the Sabbath and Yom Tov are each referred to as an אוֹת,, *a sign* between God and His people, the *tefillin* (also an אוֹת) are seen as superfluous and would thereby detract from the Sabbath or Festivals (*O.C.* 31:1).

Additionally, *tefillin* are considered *muktzah*, set aside from being used, and cannot be moved on the Sabbath and Festivals unless the place they occupy is needed or if the *tefillin* themselves will be used for a permissible function (*M.B.* 31:2).

⋖ *Tishah B'Av*

The ninth day of Av, *Tishah B'Av*, is a day of mourning for the Jewish people, commemorating the destruction of both the first and second Temples. *Tefillin* are worn during the afternoon prayers, *Minchah*, instead of *Shacharis* (*O.C.* 555:1).

⋖ *Chol HaMoed*

There are various customs regarding the wearing of *tefillin* on Chol HaMoed, the intermediate days of Passover and Succos (see

Customs). Each person should follow his own particular custom. In the event one is unsure what custom to follow, a halachic authority should be consulted.

◄§ Procedures

◄§ *Talis* First

One who wears both a *talis* and *tefillin* should put on the *talis* first. Because of the concept of אֵין מַעֲבִירִין עַל הַמִּצְוֹת, *we do not bypass one mitzvah for another*, it is proper to position the *talis* so that it is removed first each morning (*O.C.* 25:1).

The *shel yad* is likewise put on before the *shel rosh*. Proper placement of the *tefillin* in their pouch is, therefore, advisable in order to ensure that the proper sequence is followed (*O.C.* 25:5).

◄§ Which Hand?

Right-handers wear the *shel yad* on their left arm. Left-handers, whether through birth, habit or choice, place the *shel yad* on their right arm (*O.C.* 27:6). One who wears his *tefillin* on the wrong arm has not fulfilled the *mitzvah* (*M.B.* 27:24).

Someone who is *totally* ambidextrous, that is, he shows no preference in utilizing either hand in the activities he performs is considered to be right-handed and places the *shel yad* on his left arm (*M.B.* 27:25).

There is no definitive halachic stance with respect to those who write with one hand and perform all other work with the other hand. A halachic authority must be consulted in such instances.

The special prayer לְשֵׁם יִחוּד, is said and the *shel yad* is removed from the pouch with the right hand. Caution is advised when removing the *tefillah* from its covering, so that the *yud kesher*, knot shaped like a *yud*, remains touching the *bayis* and the *retzuah* does not touch the floor (*O.C.* 27:2).

It is appropriate to kiss the *bayis* before putting it on (*O.C.* 28:3).

◄§ Position

The *tefillah* is then positioned on the lower portion of the bicep of the left arm (or the right arm, if one is left-handed), tilted towards the heart, with the *ma'avarta* on top *see diagram* (*O.C.* 27:1). No material, e.g. shirt sleeve, should separate the *bayis* or

Direction of the winding (Ashkenaz)

Direction of the winding (Sephard)

*Position of the tefillin
shel rosh (front)*

*Position of the tefillin
shel rosh (back)*

retzuah from the arm (*O.C.* 27:4). The *retzuah* surrounding the bicep must not be twisted. The black side of it should face the outside (*O.C.* 27:11).

◆§ Berachos

The *retzuah* is then held with the right hand and the following *brachah* is recited *before* the *retzuah* is tightened: בָּרוּךְ אַתָּה ה' אֱלֹקֵינוּ מֶלֶךְ הָעוֹלָם אֲשֶׁר קִדְּשָׁנוּ בְּמִצְוֹתָיו וְצִוָּנוּ לְהָנִיחַ תְּפִילִין. The *retzuah* is then pulled tightly, fastening the *shel yad* in place (*O.C.* 25:5), and is then wound seven times around the lower arm (*M.B.* 27:31). The *minhag* Ashkenaz is to wind the *retzuah* towards the body; the *minhag* Sephard is to wind it away from the body (see diagram) (*Be'ur Halachah* 27:2). The end of the *retzuah* is temporarily wound around the hand (*M.B.* 25:38). No interruption of any kind, e.g. speech, gesture, or delay is permitted until after the *shel rosh* is properly positioned on one's head (*M.B.* 25:29).

The same care and caution must now be exercised in removing the *shel rosh* from the pouch and putting it on. According to all customs, everyone stands while putting the *shel rosh* on the head (*Rama* 25:11).

The correct position for the *shel rosh* is above the forehead, in a place where hair normally grows, in the center — directly above the space between the eyes (see diagram). The *dalet kesher* is placed in the center of the back of the head, just above the indentation leading to the neck *(see diagram)* (*M.B.* 27:33-35). The following *brachah* is then recited *prior* to the *retzuah* being tightened: בָּרוּךְ אַתָּה ה' אֱלֹקֵינוּ מֶלֶךְ הָעוֹלָם אֲשֶׁר קִדְּשָׁנוּ בְּמִצְוֹתָיו וְצִוָּנוּ עַל מִצְוַת תְּפִילִין.

Those of Sephardic origin do not recite this *brachah*. The *retzuah* is then tightened (*O.C.* 25:5).

Extreme care must be taken to ensure that the *bayis* of the *shel rosh* does not droop lower than the hairline or shift to the right or left . It is, therefore, essential that the *retzuah* which encircles the head be the proper size and be pulled tightly. Again, the black side must face outward (*M.B.* 27:38-39).

Immediately, after the *retzuah* is tightened, Ashkenazim say: "בָּרוּךְ שֵׁם כְּבוד מַלְכוּתוֹ לְעוֹלָם וָעֶד", in an undertone (*Rama* 25:5). The *retzuah* on both sides of the *dalet kesher* is then passed over the shoulders to hang in front of the wearer.

The verses "וּמֵחָכְמָתָךְ. . . ", (found in any *siddur*) are customarily

said at this time, concluding with the verse: „פּוֹתֵחַ אֶת יָדֶךָ וּמַשְׂבִּיעַ לְכָל חַי רָצוֹן", whose seven words correspond to the seven ties wrapped on the lower arm. Many then touch the *bayis* of each *tefillah* and kiss those fingertips.

Returning to the *shel yad*, the end of the *retzuah* is then wrapped around the middle finger three times — twice around the lowest section of the finger and once around the middle section. The verses „וְאֵרַשְׂתִּיךְ. . ." are said while doing this. Some have a custom to extend the third coil around the ring finger as well, creating a *"dalet,"* and the remaining *retzuah* portion around the hand in the shape of a *"shin"*. There are many different customs concerning how this is done. The end of the *retzuah* can then be tucked in anywhere. Some conclude by reciting the sections of „וְהָיָה כִּי יְבִיאֲךָ. . . .", and „קַדֶּשׁ לִי. . .".

The *bayis* of the *shel rosh* should be worn uncovered while the *kesher* may be covered (*O.C.* 27:11). It is preferable for the *bayis* of the *shel yad* to be covered while it is worn (*M.B.* 27:47).

✑ Interruption

If someone spoke after putting on the *shel yad*, for any reason except for the purpose of *tefillin*, he is required to move the *shel yad* out of place, recite the *brachah* „לְהָנִיחַ תְּפִילִין. . .", and return the *shel yad* to its proper position. If, for some reason, completion of the *mitzvah* cannot be accomplished without speaking, he may do so (*M.B.* 25:31-34).

Even the responses to *kaddish*, *kedushah*, or *borchu* are forbidden during the interval between putting on the *shel yad* and *shel rosh* and their respective blessings. It is, however, proper to keep silent during those times, listen to what the *chazzan* is saying and intend to fulfill his *mitzvah* as if he were actually responding (*O.C.* 25:10).

Two exceptions to this rule are Chol Hamoed and the *tefillin* of *Rabbeinu Tam*. Since no *brachos* are recited at these times, even answering אָמֵן is not considered an interruption. It is still proper, however, to move the *shel yad* out of place and then back into place in order that the *shel yad* and the *shel rosh* should be considered one unit (*M.B.* 25:36).

If someone removes his *tefillin*, a new *brachah* is required when he puts them on again — unless his intention was to put them back on immediately or unless he was in the middle of davening (*M.B.* 25:43).

If, however, while saying the original *brachah* he had the intention of removing his *tefillin* and putting them back on again, a new *brachah* is unnecessary *(ibid.)*.

If *tefillin* were removed because someone had to go to the bathroom or because of flatulence, a new *brachah* is required *(M.B. 25:47)*.

Note: Moving the *tefillin* out of place intentionally, constitutes the same action as removing them completely. Consequently, the same *halachos* apply *(O.C. 25:12)*.

Should the *tefillin* inadvertently move out of place during davening, no new *brachah* is required *(ibid.)*.

Also, no new *brachah* is ever required if one removed only one *tefillah* while keeping the other one on, and had in mind to put it back on *(Be'ur Halachah 25:12)*.

Care must be taken to ensure that no *chatzitzah*, separation, come between the *tefillin* and the body. This halachah applies to the *batim* of both the *shel yad* and the *shel rosh* and the *retzuos* of the *kesharim*. This, of course, does not apply to the *retzuos* of the *shel rosh* which hang down in front of the wearer *(O.C. 27:4)*.

It is also preferable not to allow any *chatzitzah* for the *retzuah* of the *shel yad* which is wound on the forearm and fingers *(Kaf HaChaim 27:20)*.

While the *shel yad* or its straps may, if necessary, be put on top of a cast or bandage, it should not rest on a shirt sleeve or a wrist watch.

Long hair, a wig, a *yarmulkah* and temples of eyeglasses, however, are some of the more common separations that invalidate the *mitzvah* of *tefillin shel rosh*. Similarly, someone suffering from a head injury or similar condition may, if necessary, wear his *shel rosh* over a thin covering or a bandage *(ibid.)*.

In all of these questionable circumstances, as well as the rulings regarding which *brachos* are recited in those cases, a halachic authority should be consulted.

⋅§ General Halachos

The nature of the *mitzvah* of *tefillin* is of such significance that one must constantly be aware of the *tefillin* while they are on him.

Awareness In order to facilitate this necessary state of awareness, it is advisable to touch the *tefillin* frequently, thereby also ensuring that they are in their proper place

(*M.B.* 28:1). Indeed, during davening, there are several specifically designated verses during which the *tefillin* should be touched with the fingertips. The fingertips are, thereafter, kissed (*Chayai Adam* 14:15). Some of these verses are:

1) אַשְׁרֵי in „פוֹתֵחַ אֶת יָדֶךָ וּמַשְׂבִּיעַ לְכָל חַי רָצוֹן",
You open Your hand and satisfy the desire of every living thing.

2) „בָּרוּךְ אַתָּה ה׳ אֱלֹקֵינוּ מֶלֶךְ הָעוֹלָם יוֹצֵר אוֹר וּבוֹרֵא חֹשֶׁךְ עֹשֶׂה שָׁלוֹם וּבוֹרֵא אֶת הַכֹּל"
Blessed are You, Hashem, our God, King of the Universe, Who forms light and creates darkness, makes peace and creates all.

3) קְרִיאַת שְׁמַע in „וּקְשַׁרְתָּם לְאוֹת עַל יָדֶךָ וְהָיוּ לְטֹטָפוֹת בֵּין עֵינֶיךָ"
Bind them as a sign upon your arm and let them be tefillin between your eyes.

Borrowing

Borrowing someone else's *tefillin* without permission is permissible, provided that the owner cannot be asked and that it is not done on a regular basis. Understandably, the *tefillin* must be kept in the same place they are found and must be wrapped up upon completion of their use (*M.B.* 25:53). A *brachah* may not be recited on *tefillin* which are stolen (*O.C.* 25:12).

Sanctity

Written or printed articles of holiness and sanctity cannot be brought into a lavatory. This applies to a *siddur*, a *chumash*, other holy books, a *mezuzah* and to *tefillin*. One may not relieve oneself, through defecation in the presence of these articles unless they are behind a partition approximately 40 inches high or are resting in a container which is enclosed by a second container, כְּלִי בְּתוֹךְ כְּלִי. One of these containers should not be specifically designated as a covering for the *tefillin*. Keeping the *tefillin* pouch inside the *talis* bag, for example, would not constitute an adequate enclosure. An additional covering such as a plastic bag over both of them would still be required. Even passing air is forbidden while wearing *tefillin* (*M.B.* 40:4-7). For this reason, one should avoid sleeping, even briefly, while wearing *tefillin* (*O.C.* 37:3).

If someone is carrying *tefillin* in a bag and he needs to use a public

restroom, but has no safe place to momentarily put his *tefillin*, he may place the *tefillin* bag in his pocket or wrap them in his own garment while using the lavatory (*M.B.* 43:24).

Out of respect for the sanctity of the *tefillin* it is also improper to eat or drink while wearing *tefillin*. Similarly, one should refrain from handling unclean objects, such as soiled diapers while wearing *tefillin*.

Wearing *tefillin* near graves or in a room where a deceased person is present, is also prohibited (*O.C.* 45:1).

Tefillin should be taken off before the *talis* is removed (*Kitzur Shulchan Aruch* 10:20).

Removal of Tefillin

It is best to leave the *tefillin* on until after the final *kaddish* (after עָלֵינוּ) of *Shacharis*. If necessary, one may remove them after the *kaddish* which follows וּבָא לְצִיוֹן, and, if most pressing, following the *kedushah* in חֲזָרַת הַשַ״ץ — the repetition of *Shemoneh Esrei*. During *kaddish* itself, however, one should refrain from taking off the *tefillin*, concentrating fully on answering אָמֵן יְהֵא שְׁמֵיה רַבָּא וכו׳. . . and the rest of *kaddish* (*M.B.* 25:56).

In cases where the *Sefer Torah* is awaiting its return to the Ark, the removal of the *tefillin* should be delayed until the Torah is properly put away. In no situation should the *tefillin* be removed in front of the *Sefer Torah*. If there is no recourse, one should move to a distance far from the Torah and remove the *tefillin* while not facing the Torah directly (*O.C.* 25:13; *M.B.* 57-58).

These laws apply to removal of the *shel rosh*. While both *tefillin* should preferably not be removed until after *Shacharis*, the *shel yad*, if necessary, can be removed in front of a *Sefer Torah (ibid.)*.

The procedure for removing the *tefillin* is as follows: First, the coils of *shel yad retzuah* are unwound from the fingers and are wrapped around the palm. Second, the *shel rosh* is removed with the weaker hand (the hand with the *shel yad* still wound on it) and is wound up and placed in the *tefillin* pouch on the right side. Finally, the *shel yad* is removed, wound up, and placed in the left side of the *tefillin* pouch (*M.B.* 28:5-6,9).

Except for Sephardim, who sit while putting on and taking off the *shel yad*, everyone else stands during the entire removal process (*O.C.* 28:2).

It is considered proper to kiss the *batim* of the *tefillin* before and after wearing them (*O.C.* 28:3).

When wrapping the *retzuos*, they should be wrapped over the sides of the *bayis*, around the *titurah* — not on top of the *bayis*. Some have the custom to wrap the *retzuos* on both sides of the *titurah* to resemble the wings of a dove (*M.B.* 28:9). Others wrap the *retzuos* differently. It is also customary to place the *kesher*, the knot, of the *shel rosh* on the *maavarta* and not below it, since the *dalet* it forms is a letter in Hashem's name (*Aruch HaShulchan* 28:68).

Circumcision

When a *bris*, circumcision, is to be performed in *shul* right after *Shacharis*, it is preferable for one to keep his *tefillin* on until after the *bris* (*M.B.* 25:55; See also *Igros Moshe O.C.* Vol. IV, chap. 101 note 4).

Rosh Chodesh

On Rosh Chodesh, the *tefillin* are removed immediately following the *kaddish* which precedes *Mussaf*. If, by mistake, one started *Mussaf* with his *tefillin* on, he may not remove them until he has completed the *Shemoneh Esrei* (*M.B.* 25:61).

Those who wear *tefillin* on Chol Hamoed should remove them before *Hallel* (*M.B.* 25:60).

Sanctity of Tefillin

Tefillin, at all times, must be treated with great respect, since they are articles of immense holiness. One should exercise great care with his *tefillin* — making sure that when they are not being worn, they are kept in a secure pouch and in a safe place.

If, God forbid, the *tefillin* should fall to the floor while they were not in a bag or pouch, the custom is to designate a day for fasting as an atonement for his careless treatment. Even if the *tefillin* were in their pouch when they fell, some atonement is still indicated. This usually takes the form of contributing some money to charity, *tzedakah*. Many are of the opinion that giving *tzedakah* is adequate atonement in either case — if fasting is especially difficult (*M.B.* 40:3, see also *Kaf HaChaim* 40:5).

Those who desire to exercise an added degree of caution, are careful never to put on or take off their *tefillin* unless there is a table directly beneath the *tefillin*.

Even sitting on a bench upon which *tefillin* are also laying, is considered disrespectful, and is prohibited. If the *tefillin* are raised a

tefach, a handbreadth, approximately 4 inches, it is permissible (*Teshuvos Radvaz* vol. III, chap. 515).

No part of the *shel rosh* — not a *retzuah*, a *parshah*, or even the cover — can be used for a *shel yad* because the *shel rosh*, containing the *shin* and the *dalet kesher,* contains greater sanctity than the *shel yad.* Changing a *shel yad* into a *shel rosh* is, therefore, permissible (*O.C.* 42:1).

Even the *tefillin* pouch contains a certain measure of holiness. If the bag was permanently designated for *tefillin* use and *tefillin* were

The Pouch

actually kept there (even once), it is forbidden to use that bag for any other purpose. When it is no longer useful it cannot be discarded. Like other articles or printed matter which are holy, the bag must be placed in *shaymos*, for eventual burial. It is not even proper to place a *siddur* in the *tefillin* pouch. Putting the *siddur* in a plastic bag into which the *tefillin* bag is placed, is appropriate. That plastic bag has no inherent sanctity and may, eventually, be discarded (*O.C.* 42:3; *M.B.* 16).

Because of the exacting requirements deemed necessary to maintain *tefillin* which are kosher, it is prudent to examine them externally on

Care and Maintenance

a periodic basis. Potential problem areas should be visually inspected to be certain that no invalidation has already, or might soon develop. One should, therefore, attain the habit of viewing the *retzuos* to be sure that their blackness remains intact and that their width is correct. Similarly, the *batim* should be examined to ensure that the corners have not become rounded (*M.B.* 32:181, 27:42).

All *tefillin*, regardless of the frequency of their use, should be professionally inspected, by a *sofer*, certified scribe, twice in seven years (*M.B.* 39:27).

Immediate inspection is required if the *tefillin* became wet or if a tear develops in one of the *batim*. If a *sofer* is unavailable to inspect the *tefillin*, one should borrow someone else's in the interim. If that arrangement is not feasible, it is best to wear one's own *tefillin* without making a *brachah* (*M.B.* 39:26).

RITUAL OBSERVANCE

ברכות ההפטרה

קדס קריאת ההפטרה יברך

וטעם קריאת ההפטרה כתב הר"ד
אבודרהם ז"ל, ולמה מפטירין בנביאים
לפי שגזרו שמד על ישראל שלא יקראו
בתורה וכנגד ז' שהיו עולין לקרות בתורה

ואין קורין פחות מכ"א פסוקים לכל א' וא' תקנו
לקרות כ"א פסוקים בנביאים ואם נשלם הענין בפחות
מכ"א פסוקים כגון הפטרת שובה אין צריך לקרות יותר
ולכן נקראת ההפטרה לפי שהיו נפטרין בה ממקרא עכ"ל

בָּרוּךְ אַתָּה יְיָ אֱלֹהֵינוּ מֶלֶךְ הָעוֹלָם אֲשֶׁר בָּחַר בִּנְבִיאִים טוֹבִים וְרָצָה בְדִבְרֵיהֶם הַנֶּאֱמָרִים בֶּאֱמֶת. בָּרוּךְ אַתָּה יְיָ הַבּוֹחֵר בַּתּוֹרָה וּבְמשֶׁה עַבְדּוֹ וּבְיִשְׂרָאֵל עַמּוֹ וּבִנְבִיאֵי הָאֱמֶת וָצֶדֶק:

ברכות אחר ההפטרה

נֶאֱמָן אַתָּה הוּא יְיָ אֱלֹהֵינוּ וְנֶאֱמָנִים דְּבָרֶיךָ וְדָבָר אֶחָד מִדְּבָרֶיךָ אָחוֹר לֹא יָשׁוּב רֵיקָם כִּי אֵל מֶלֶךְ נֶאֱמָן וְרַחֲמָן אָתָּה. בָּרוּךְ אַתָּה יְיָ הָאֵל הַנֶּאֱמָן בְּכָל דְּבָרָיו:

בָּרוּךְ אַתָּה יְיָ אֱלֹהֵינוּ מֶלֶךְ הָעוֹלָם צוּר כָּל הָעוֹלָמִים צַדִּיק בְּכָל הַדּוֹרוֹת הָאֵל הַנֶּאֱמָן הָאוֹמֵר וְעֹשֶׂה הַמְדַבֵּר וּמְקַיֵּם שֶׁכָּל דְּבָרָיו אֱמֶת וָצֶדֶק. נֶאֱמָן אַתָּה הוּא

שַׂמְּחֵנוּ יְיָ אֱלֹהֵינוּ בְּאֵלִיָּהוּ הַנָּבִיא עַבְדֶּךָ וּבְמַלְכוּת בֵּית דָּוִד מְשִׁיחֶךָ בִּמְהֵרָה יָבֹא וְיָגֵל לִבֵּנוּ עַל כִּסְאוֹ לֹא יֵשֵׁב זָר וְלֹא יִנְחֲלוּ עוֹד אֲחֵרִים אֶת כְּבוֹדוֹ כִּי בְשֵׁם קָדְשְׁךָ נִשְׁבַּעְתָּ לּוֹ שֶׁלֹּא יִכְבֶּה נֵרוֹ לְעוֹלָם וָעֶד. בָּרוּךְ אַתָּה יְיָ מָגֵן דָּוִד:

כשחל אחד מן הימים טובים
בשבת קדש א"א מוסיפים את
המלים הנכלאים בסוגריים

עַל הַתּוֹרָה וְעַל הָעֲבוֹדָה וְעַל הַנְּבִיאִים וְעַל יוֹם הַשַּׁבָּת הַזֶּה (וְיוֹם

לפסח חַג הַמַּצּוֹת לשבועות חַג הַשָּׁבוּעוֹת

לסכות חַג הַסֻּכּוֹת לשמע"צ השמיני חַג הָעֲצֶרֶת ולש"ת הַזֶּה) שֶׁנָּתַתָּ לָּנוּ יְיָ אֱלֹהֵינוּ לִקְדֻשָּׁה וְלִמְנוּחָה (לְשָׂשׂוֹן וּלְשִׂמְחָה) לְכָבוֹד וּלְתִפְאָרֶת. עַל הַכֹּל יְיָ אֱלֹהֵינוּ אֲנַחְנוּ מוֹדִים לָךְ וּמְבָרְכִים אוֹתָךְ יִתְבָּרַךְ שִׁמְךָ בְּפִי כָּל חַי תָּמִיד לְעוֹלָם וָעֶד. בָּרוּךְ אַתָּה יְיָ מְקַדֵּשׁ הַשַּׁבָּת (וְיִשְׂרָאֵל וְהַזְּמַנִּים):

כִּי הִיא בֵּית חַיֵּינוּ וּלְעֲלוּבַת נֶפֶשׁ תּוֹשִׁיעַ בִּמְהֵרָה בְיָמֵינוּ. בָּרוּךְ אַתָּה יְיָ מְשַׂמֵּחַ צִיּוֹן בְּבָנֶיהָ:

בִּרְכוֹת הַתּוֹרָה

בָּרְכוּ אֶת יְיָ הַמְבֹרָךְ:

קהל בָּרוּךְ יְיָ הַמְבֹרָךְ לְעוֹלָם וָעֶד: ‏יחזור ומצרך

בָּרוּךְ אַתָּה יְיָ אֱלֹהֵינוּ מֶלֶךְ הָעוֹלָם אֲשֶׁר בָּחַר בָּנוּ מִכָּל ‏לא עשה כן‏ ‏לכל גוי‏ הָעַמִּים וְנָתַן לָנוּ אֶת תּוֹרָתוֹ. בָּרוּךְ אַתָּה יְיָ נוֹתֵן הַתּוֹרָה:

אמר כאן ג׳ דברים כנגד ג׳ פעמים שקבלו עליהם ישראל התורה א׳ כשאמר והייתם לי סגולה קבלו עליהם כל המלות
ופעם ב׳ כשעמד משה הנביא לכך רמז בצרכה זו כל ג׳ הנ"ל אשר בחר בנו הוא והייתם לי
סגולה ונתן לנו את תורתו הוא מעמד הר סיני שקבלו התורה מפיו של הקב"ה נותן התורה הוא בזה׳ הידיעה הוא נגד
תורה שבע"פ שקבלנו ממשה רבנו ע"פ ועל פה אמר לשון בינוני נותן כי ידיעת תורה שבעל פה מתחדש בידיעה תמיד (אצני אליהו)

ואחר הקריאה יצרך:

בָּרוּךְ אַתָּה יְיָ אֱלֹהֵינוּ מֶלֶךְ הָעוֹלָם אֲשֶׁר נָתַן לָנוּ תּוֹרַת אֱמֶת ‏זו תורה שבכתב‏ וְחַיֵּי עוֹלָם נָטַע בְּתוֹכֵנוּ. ‏זו תורה שבעל פה‏ בָּרוּךְ אַתָּה יְיָ נוֹתֵן הַתּוֹרָה:

מי שהגיע בנו לבן י"ג שנה ויום אחד יברך האב בשעה שבנו עולה לתורה פעם ראשונה, בלא שם ומלכות

בָּרוּךְ שֶׁפְּטָרַנִי מֵעָנְשׁוּ שֶׁלָּזֶה:

Blessings on the *Torah*

The right panel pictures pictures the two Tablets of the Law, given by God as Mount Sinai was enveloped in flames. The blessing thanks God for having chosen us from among the nations of the world. The second blessing, said after the portion of the Torah has been read, praises God Who gave us the Torah of truth, referring to the Written Law, and implanted eternal life within us, referring to the Oral Law.

The Vilna Gaon explains the first blessing as the three distinct facets in our receiving the Torah. "Who has chosen us from among the nations", refers to the exalted status achieved by our nation by virtue of our willingness to accept the Torah. The second phase refers to the Revelation at Sinai, when God spoke directly to us. The third facet is the Oral Law transmittrd by Moses to the Jewish People, an ongoing transmission.

The blessing at the bottom of the plate, is the baruch she'petarani, said by the father of the bar mitzvah boy after he has completed his first aliyah.

Blessings for the *Haftarah*

The five blessings recited, one before and four after the reading of the haftarah, correspond to the Five Books of Moses. During times of persecution when Jews were not allowed to read the Torah in public, they would read from the Prophets to exempt one from the reading of the Torah. The word haftarah means exemption (Abudraham).

The first blessing extols God's Omnipotence, as it were, in being the "Rock of all worlds." This world, created with a ה, hei, mirrors the heavenly Jerusalem created with a י, yud. The second blessing, רַחֵם עַל צִיוֹן, beseeches God to have mercy on Zion, home of the Holy Temple. We all await the shofar's sound by the Prophet Elijah, when a King of the House of David will return to David's throne. The last panel depicts Sabbath as the central theme, with symbols of Succos, Simchas Torah, Shavuos and Pesach adorning the panel as well.

RITUAL לשם OBSERVANCE דקדוקים

✥ *Seudah:* The Festive *Bar Mitzvah* Meal

o acknowledge the great joy which accompanies the entry of a boy into the *bar mitzvah* fraternity, there is a *mitzvah* for a father to arrange a special *seudah*, festive meal, to mark the occasion (*M.B.* 225:6 in the name of *Magen Avraham*). It is at this gathering that a father demonstrates his appreciation and expresses words of gratitude to God for allowing his son to reach this coveted state of sanctity. Articulating thanks for having been given the privilege of raising and educating his son and for witnessing this most memorable event, is also appropriate for the father at this time (*Yam Shel Shlomo, Bava Kamma* chap. 7 note 37).

Indeed, our Sages tell us that the joy experienced by the father during the *bar mitzvah* of one's son is comparable to the happiness he feels on his sons's wedding day. The *Tanna*, Rabbi Shimon bar Yochai was jubilant on the day his son, Rabbi Elazar, became a *bar mitzvah*. He decorated his entire house with beautiful ornaments and celebrated for three days (*Zohar Chadash, Genesis* 110:2 and 11:1).

It is, therefore, quite apparent that this festive occasion marks the arrival of a significant spiritual moment in a child's life and should, in no way, resemble an ordinary birthday party. All celebration particulars, including invitations, attire, ambience, food, entertainment, and program content, should reflect and enhance the holy nature of this sacred day. Long after the helium-filled balloons have shriveled and succumbed to gravity, the ever-lasting images of *kedushah*, pure holiness, should remain embedded in the soul of the *bar mitzvah* boy and of his celebrants.

RITUAL
OBSERVANCE
לשם שיר וקלים

☐ If at all possible, the meal should convene on the very day (or evening) of the boy's *bar mitzvah*. If this is not feasible, an alternate day, soon after, may be selected. Nevertheless, regardless of when the meal is actually celebrated, it is still considered to be a *seudas mitzvah* if the *bar mitzvah* boy addresses the guests with a Torah discourse (see *Pshet'l* section) (*Yam shel Shlomo, loc. cit.* and *M.B. loc. cit.*).

☐ The *seudah* can take place on the Sabbath, or on a Festival, or on *Purim* or Chol HaMoed, whether or not it is the actual *bar mitzvah* day. Planning the meal for *Rosh Hashanah*, if that is not the true *bar mitzvah* day, however, is not in keeping with the spirit of awe and reverence that must be upheld on those two days (*Matteh Ephraim* 596:5).

☐ If a boy's *bar mitzvah* date falls on the day before the Sabbath or Festivals, no postponement is necessary. These days should not be selected as alternatives for the actual *bar mitzvah* date since it is generally forbidden to designate a special meal on those days (*Aruch HaShulchan O.C.* 249:7, *O.C.* 249:2 and *Rama ibid.*).

☐ The *seudah* for a *bar mitzvah* which falls on a Friday or on the eve of *Shavuous* should be held before noon, if possible (*M.B.* 249:13). If necessary it could begin any time before the beginning of the tenth hour of the day — approximately 3:00 P.M. standard time (*ibid.*).

☐ The *bar mitzvah seudah* on the eve of *Succos*, can begin any time before the tenth hour of the day (*M.B.* 639:27).

☐ A *bar mitzvah* occurring on Passover eve should be held prior to the time that *chametz*, leavened bread, can no longer be eaten (*M.B.* 471:21).

☐ If the *bar mitzvah* date falls on *Yom Kippur* or *Tishah B'Av*, the *seudah* is held at night, after the fast. Meat and wine may be served at a *bar mitzvah seudah* which is held the night after *Tishah B'Av*, although they are generally prohibited until after midday of the tenth of *Av*. The *seudah* for a boy whose *bar mitzvah* date is on any other public fast day, (e.g. the *Fast of Esther*, the 17th day of *Tammuz* etc.) may be scheduled for the evening prior to the fast or immediately following the fast.

☐ The celebration for a *bar mitzvah* which falls during the nine day mourning period prior to *Tishah B'Av* may include meat and wine. *Bar mitzvahs* during the *sefirah* period — between *Passover* and *Shavuos* — should be celebrated without music.

□ The *bar mitzvah seudah* may be combined with any other festive celebration of a *mitzvah,* such as the completion of a tractate in the Talmud or the writing of a *sefer Torah.* It is appropriate to designate a special food, in such a case, to represent the joy of the second *simchah* (*Minchas Yitzchak* vol. IV, chap. 23).

□ Regarding the attendance and customs of those in a mourning period in reference to a *bar mitzvah*, there are varying opinions. A halachic authority should be consulted.

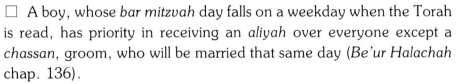

ᴇ§ *Aliyah L'Torah*

The first reference found regarding the *bar mitzvah* boy being called to the Torah to receive an *aliyah* is in the Gaonic era — the 8th century. R' Yehudai Gaon is reported to have recited the special blessing *"Boruch She'petarani"* at the time of his son's first *aliyah* (*Orchos Chaim* p. 43 *Hilchos Berachos,* chap. 58).

□ A boy, whose *bar mitzvah* day falls on a weekday when the Torah is read, has priority in receiving an *aliyah* over everyone except a *chassan*, groom, who will be married that same day (*Be'ur Halachah* chap. 136).

□ On the Sabbath, equal priority is given to a *bar mitzvah* boy whose *bar mitzvah* occurred any day that week and a *chasan* who will be married in the forthcoming week. If necessary, lots should be drawn to determine who receives the *aliyah* priority (*ibid.*). Some might only consider the *bar mitzvah* boy to be on equal footing with the *chasan*, if that Sabbath was actually his *bar mitzvah* day (*Shaarei Ephraim chap. 62*)

□ If a boy's *bar mitzvah* day falls on a weekday, various customs exist regarding when he should receive his *aliyah l'Torah*.

There is an opinion that one's first *aliyah* should be on the Sabbath, regardless of the actual day he became a *bar mitzvah* (*Shvus Yaakov vol.* II; chap. 129).

The renowned *Ba'al Ha'Tanya*, R' Shneur Zalman of Liadi arranged for his son to receive his first *aliyah* on Sabbath afternoon, even though his actual *bar mitzvah* date was two days earlier, on Thursday (*Likutei Deburim M'Lubavitch, Shevat 5696*).

Others believe that if one's *bar mitzvah* date coincides with a Torah reading (e.g. Monday, Thursday, Chol Ha'Moed, a public fast day), the *aliyah* should be given on that day (*Shaarei Ephraim,* chap. 2, note 2).

RITUAL שֶׁל
OBSERVANCE וּבְקִים

There is even a custom that the *bar mitzvah* boy receive his initial *aliyah* at *Maftir* of the previous Sabbath, and his second *aliyah* the following Sabbath (*Tzitz Eliezer* vol. 7 chap. 1). Clearly, one must follow his particular custom or ask a competent Rabbinic authority. (See p. 115).

☐ As to which *aliyah* the *bar mitzvah* boy should be given, differing opinions exist. According to certain authorities, the *bar mitzvah* boy may receive any *aliyah* except for *Maftir*, since from a purely halachic stand-point there is no objection to even a minor being called up for *Maftir* (*M.B.* 282:12). The prevailing custom, however, is for the *bar mitzvah* boy to receive the *Maftir aliyah*. A competent rabbi should confirm this plan prior to any definitive arrangements being made (see p. 115).

☐ While it has become customary for the father of the *bar mitzvah* boy to receive an *aliyah*, it is by no means obligatory.

☐ It is considered to be an honor and a privilege to read the Torah portion aloud for the congregation and many *bar mitzvah* boys avail themselves of this opportunity. Even among those who do not read the entire *sidra*, Torah portion, on the Sabbath of their *bar mitzvah*, most do read the *Maftir*, the final few verses of the *parshah*, and the *haftarah,* the weekly reading from the Prophets which follows the Biblical reading.

☐ The possible exceptions to this, might be the *maftir* readings of *Parshas Zachor* and *Parshas Parah*. These commandments may be Biblical in origin and may thus, require the reader to have acquired all the requisite physical characteristics of an adult. This includes the growth of at least two pubic hairs. To avoid investigation and any potential embarrassment, an older person is asked to read *Parshas Zachor (Tzitz Eliezer ibid.)*.

☐ If two *bar mitzvah* boys are present in one congregation on the same Sabbath, and both express a desire to read the *haftarah*, lots should be drawn to determine who should read. It is not permitted for both boys to read the *haftarah* together or to divide the *haftarah* and allow each boy to read a part. Reading *haftarah* blessings together or dividing them is likewise not permissible (*Rama, O.C.* 284:5; see also *Igros Moshe O.C.* chap. 102).

☐ Under certain circumstances where both parties adamantly refuse to draw lots, the congregation may be permitted to form two distinct services in different locations and conduct separate Torah readings and *haftarah* reading services. This alternative should be implemented only with Rabbinic sanction (*Tzitz Eliezer* vol. VI, chap. 36).

☐ A *bar mitzvah* boy who is blind may receive an *aliyah* but may not "read" from the Torah, since the Torah may not be recited publicly by heart. Conversely, the *haftarah* may be read by heart, although utilization of a braille text is preferable. This is so only in synagogues where the practice of reading the *haftarah* from a parchment scroll is not followed (see the pamphlet *"Be'inyan Krias Hahaftarah Be'al Peh,* London, by Dayan Avraham Rapaport, 1961).

◦§ *Baruch She'petarani*

The father of a *bar mitzvah* boy recites the following blessing after the boy completes his first *aliyah* to the Torah:

"Baruch she'petarani me'onsho shelazeh."[1]

"Blessed is the One who has freed me from the punishment due this boy."

The source of this blessing is the *Midrash Rabbah* to *Genesis* 25:27, which describes the development of Jacob and Esau, *"VaYigdalu Ha'niarim."*

There are two possible interpretations for this blessing:

1) Until this time a father, being fully responsible for the education of his son, would be liable for the punishments resulting from the sins incurred by his son. In becoming a *bar mitzvah*, the son, who is now personally responsible, removes this burden from his father.

2) Alternatively, until this time a child under *bar mitzvah* might suffer punishment for the sins of his father. The father's blessing is therefore a proclamation of gratitude for no longer being the source of his son's punishment (*Magen Avraham,* O.C. 225, note 5, in the name of *Levush*).[2]

☐ The prevailing custom is for the father to accompany his son at the time of his first *aliyah* to the Torah and to recite the blessing immediately after his son completes his final blessing on the Torah:

---

1. The cited form of the blessing omits the name of God, as do most congregations. There are, however, some Rabbinic authorities (among them the *Vilna Gaon*), who rule that the blessing should be recited in its full form, that is, with the *Name* of God.

2. Indeed, Rav Boruch Epstein, in *Baruch She'amar*, declares that because of the foregoing reason it would actually be more appropriate for the *son* to recite the blessing. This custom is not commonly followed. (See also *Shach Al HaTorah, Lech Lecha*).

RITUAL OBSERVANCE לשמר ולקיים

בָּרוּךְ אַתָּה ה׳ אֱלֹקֵינוּ מֶלֶךְ הָעוֹלָם, אֲשֶׁר נָתַן לָנוּ תּוֹרַת אֱמֶת, וְחַיֵּי עוֹלָם נָטַע בְּתוֹכֵנוּ. בָּרוּךְ אַתָּה ה׳, נוֹתֵן הַתּוֹרָה.

Blessed are You, HASHEM, our God, King of the Universe, Who gave us the Torah of truth and implanted eternal life within us. Blessed are You, HASHEM, Giver of the Torah.

☐ The blessing could also be recited when the *bar mitzvah* boy leads the congregation in prayer as a *shliach tzibbur*, since that privilege is extended only to those who are of *bar mitzvah* age.

☐ There are those who recite the blessing during the festive *bar mitzvah* meal if no Torah reading takes place that day . In any case it is preferable that no more than three days pass after one's *bar mitzvah* before the blessing is recited (*Tzitz Eliezer*, Part VII, chap. 23).

☐ At least ten people (including the *bar mitzvah* boy and his father) should be present at the time of the blessing (*ibid.; see also Divrei Malkiel*, Part I, chap. 4). If, for some reason the father and son are in different locations on the *bar mitzvah* day, the father should recite the blessing anyway, modifying it by saying: *"Boruch she'petarani me'ansho shel benee (insert son's name)."*

☐ If a *bar mitzvah* boy has no father, or if the father cannot recite the blessing for some reason, it is questionable whether the grandfather should recite the blessing. A halachic authority should be consulted (see *Maharsham*, quoted in *Sha'arei Chaim* on *Sha'arei Ephraim*, chap. 4, note 24).

☐ A father should not recite the blessing when his daughter reaches *bas mitzvah*, twelve years old (see p. 103), since according to many authorities the *chinuch* obligation of Torah education is not incumbent on a father for his daughter (*Nazir* 29a).

"Stop That Pshet'l!"
Many ask, "Why is there a custom in certain circles for the audience to interrupt the bar mitzvah boy by singing during his pshet'l, Torah discourse?"
One possible explanation is that this interruption may actually be instructive. This custom teaches him right from the beginning, that things will not always go his way. By giving the floor to others, he learns humility and patience.
— R' Aaron of Belz, זצ״ל

❧ *Pshet'l*

I t is common practice in nearly all Jewish communities for a *bar mitzvah* boy to deliver a *pshet'l*, Torah discourse, as a part of the *bar mitzvah* celebration (*Yam shel Shlomo, Bava Kamma* 87:37).

The various customs related to this meaningful ritual are discussed on pp. 117-118.

A sample discourse is presented here as an example of what a *pshet'l* can contain. A wide array of subject matter, however, is available to be selected from, for appropriate *pshet'l* application.

Sample Pshet'l

The Bar Mitzvah Discourse
   In preparation for the day of his bar mitzvah, the young man is tutored by a rabbi or teacher to deliver a pshet'l, Talmudic discourse. This classic painting by Moritz Daniel Oppenheim, a German artist (1800-1882) is from "Pictures of Traditional Jewish Family Life, which captured the warmth and imagery of life of the Jews in Germany during the nineteenth century. The bar mitzvah boy, having prepared for the occasion, is shown delivering his lecture in the family living room to his father and mother and assembled guests.
   — *Photograph, Courtesy: Israel Museum, Jerusalem*

The Shema is the Jew's daily declaration of God's Unity, Uniqueness and Indivisibility. By reciting the Shema, a Jew accepts upon himself עוֹל מַלְכוּת שָׁמַיִם, God's absolute sovereignty, and subordinates himself to God's will. Since the mitzvah of reciting Shema becomes effective at nightfall — the precise moment when a boy becomes an adult on his thirteenth birthday — the recitation of Shema is the first mitzvah for which a new Jewish adult becomes scripturally obligated. For this reason, I have selected the subject of the Shema for my bar mitzvah pshet'l.

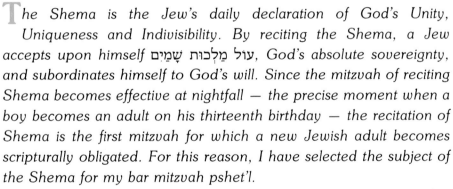

   The first two paragraphs of the Shema discuss — among other topics — the mitzvah of loving God. In the first paragraph we read: וְאָהַבְתָּ אֵת ה׳ אֱלֹקֶיךָ בְּכָל לְבָבְךָ וּבְכָל נַפְשְׁךָ וּבְכָל מְאֹדֶךָ, *You shall love Hashem, your God, with all your heart, with all your soul and with all your resources.* In the second paragraph this is reiterated: לְאַהֲבָה אֶת ה׳ אֱלֹקֵיכֶם וּלְעָבְדוֹ בְּכָל לְבַבְכֶם וּבְכָל נַפְשְׁכֶם, *to love Hashem your God, and to serve Him, with all your hearts and all your souls.* While these two verses are very similar, there is a striking difference between them. The first paragraph commands us to love God in three ways, with our hearts, our souls, and our resources. The second paragraph, mentions only the first two ways; בְּכל מְאֹדֶךָ, *with all your resources,*

RITUAL
לשמר
OBSERVANCE
ולקיים

is strangely omitted. Why does the Torah not command the Jew to love God with all his resources in the second paragraph, just as it commands him in the first one?

To answer this question we must analyze the Talmud's statement in tractate Berachos 35b. The Talmud there records a dispute between R' Yishmael and R' Shimon bar Yochai. According to R' Yishmael, although one is obligated to study Torah constantly, as God commanded Joshua: "לֹא יָמוּשׁ סֵפֶר הַתּוֹרָה הַזֶּה מִפִּיךָ, this Sefer Torah should not withdraw from Your mouth," nonetheless, one is permitted to earn a livelihood. It is only after one earns a living, that one is obligated to spend all additional free time studying Torah. R' Yishmael supports his position with a verse in the second paragraph of Shema: וְאָסַפְתָּ דְגָנֶךָ, you may gather in your grain. These words prove that God allows man to till the soil and earn a livelihood.

R' Shimon ben Yochai disputes this position. He says: אֶפְשָׁר אָדָם חוֹרֵשׁ בִּשְׁעַת חֲרִישָׁה וְזוֹרֵעַ בִּשְׁעַת זְרִיעָה וְקוֹצֵר בִּשְׁעַת קְצִירָה וְדָשׁ בִּשְׁעָה דִישָׁה וְזוֹרֶה בִּשְׁעַת הָרוּחַ תּוֹרָה מַה תְּהֵא עָלֶיהָ, if man will be occupied with plowing, seeding, harvesting, threading, and winnowing, when will Torah be studied? How will man achieve excellence in Torah scholarship? Therefore, R' Shimon bar Yochai states: בִּזְמַן שֶׁיִּשְׂרָאֵל עוֹשִׂין רְצוֹנוֹ שֶׁל מָקוֹם מְלַאכְתָּן נַעֲשִׂית עַל יְדֵי אֲחֵרִים, when a Jew does the will of God, his work will be performed by others, and he will not have to earn a living. God will provide sustenance so that he can devote himself completely to Torah study. But, asks R' Shimon bar Yochai, how then do we interpret the verse: וְאָסַפְתָּ דְגָנֶךָ, you may gather in your grain which clearly implies that man should earn his own living? R' Shimon ben Yochai answers that this verse refers to those people who do not do the will of God, אֵין עוֹשִׂין רְצוֹנוֹ שֶׁל מָקוֹם, Since they do not conduct their lives according to God's will, God does not provide a livelihood for them.

The Talmud concludes by stating: הַרְבֵּה עָשׂוּ כְּר׳ שִׁמְעוֹן בֶּן יוֹחַאי וְלֹא עָלְתָה בְּיָדָם, many tried to follow the lifestyle of R' Shimon bar Yochai but were unsuccessful. The commentaries explain this to mean that only rare individuals who have complete commitment to God can be successful in following R' Shimon ben Yochai's prescription of being totally immersed in the study of Torah, while God provides for the physical needs of the individual.

Indeed, R' Shimon ben Yochai himself practiced what he preached. The Talmud (Shabbos 31b) relates that he and his son studied Torah while they were forced to live in a cave. God provided for their physical needs for thirteen years. The community at large, however, is not on this high spiritual plane, and hence must earn their own livelihood.

R' Shimon ben Yochai's interpretation of the phrase וְאָסַפְתָּ דְגָנֶךָ, you may gather in your grain, however, demands further scrutiny. Tosafos are troubled by R' Shimon's declaration that this phrase refers only to those who do not conform to the will of God. It is that weakness, said R' Shimon, that results in their not meriting the privilege of having God provide for their physical needs. How can this be, ask Tosafos? The words: וְאָסַפְתָּ דְגָנֶךָ, you may gather in your grain, are found in the second paragraph of שְׁמַע, which also implores you: לְאַהֲבָה אֶת ה' אֱלֹקֵיכֶם בְּכָל לְבַבְכֶם וּבְכָל נַפְשְׁכֶם, to love God with all your heart and all your soul. Clearly, one who loves God with his entire heart and soul is one who does the will of God. How can R' Shimon ben Yochai maintain that וְאָסַפְתָּ דְגָנֶךָ, which is found in this very same paragraph, refers to one who does not do the will of God?

The Maharsha answers this question by referring to the distinction between the first two paragraphs of the Shema. In the second paragraph, the Torah speaks of loving God with one's entire heart and soul, but omits בְּכָל מְאֹדֶךָ — with all your resources, mentioned in the first paragraph. The second paragraph of Shema must, therefore, be referring to someone who indeed loves God with his entire heart, but has one ingredient missing. He is not willing to place total trust in God, by devoting himself completely to Torah study and foregoing the security provided by material wealth. This person loves God but wants to enjoy the wealth of this world at the same time. Because this person fails to love God בְּכָל מְאֹדֶךָ, with all his resources, R' Shimon ben Yochai refers to him as אֵין עוֹשִׂין רְצוֹנוֹ שֶׁל מָקוֹם, not doing the will of God. True, he loves God dearly with all his heart and soul, but he loves materialism as well. Such a person is not a complete servant of God.

Let us now return to our original question. Why, indeed, does the first paragraph of Shema speak of loving God with our entire wealth — while the second paragraph omits this concept? A possible explanation might be that the first paragraph of Shema is written in the singular form, e.g. בְּכָל לְבָבְךָ because it refers only to an individual. The second paragraph of Shema is written in plural form, e.g. — בְּכָל לְבַבְכֶם, with all your hearts because it refers to the entire community.

As mentioned earlier, many people tried to follow R' Shimon ben

Yochai and were unsuccessful. They did not succeed, explains the Maharsha, because they lacked the quality of loving God with all their resources, and therefore they were in the category of not doing the will of God. In the community at large, most people have not attained this lofty level of loving God with all their wealth. It is only few and rare individuals such as R' Shimon ben Yochai himself, who were able to love God to that degree. Therefore, many who tried to follow R' Shimon ben Yochai were unsuccessful.

The first paragraph of Shema, however, is written in the singular because it addresses itself to the potential that an individual can reach: — וְאָהַבְתָּ אֵת ה׳ אֱלֹקֶיךָ בְּכָל לְבָבְךָ וּבְכָל נַפְשְׁךָ וּבְכָל מְאֹדֶךָ, you shall love Hashem, your God with all your heart, with all your soul and with all your resources. In contrast, the second paragraph is written in plural. It addresses itself to the entire community. It speaks to the majority of people who have not reached the level of disdaining material wealth. It addresses the people who work for a living, as it states: וְאָסַפְתָּ דְגָנֶיךָ, you may gather in your grain. These people cannot merit the blessing of R' Shimon ben Yochai that they may study Torah while God provides sustenance, because they are not עוֹשִׂין רְצוֹנוֹ שֶׁל מָקוֹם, they do not do the will of God. Therefore, in the second paragraph of Shema, the Torah omits בְּכָל מְאֹדֶךָ, with all your resources for this is beyond the grasp of the majority of people. Only in the first portion, which speaks to the individual, does the Torah speak of the ideal way to love God — בְּכָל לְבָבְךָ וּבְכָל נַפְשְׁךָ וּבְכָל מְאֹדֶךָ.

I hope that as I grow and mature, I will be able to rise above the masses and achieve the ideal of וְאָהַבְתָּ אֵת ה׳ אֱלֹקֶיךָ בְּכָל לְבָבְךָ וּבְכָל נַפְשְׁךָ וּבְכָל מְאֹדֶךָ. In that way, I can become a source of nachas to my parents, grandparents, teachers and friends who have guided me along the path of Torah and Yiras Shamayim.

Compiled by: Rabbi Yaakov David Luban
Congregation Ohr Torah
Edison, New Jersey

BAS
MITZVAH

Bas Mitzvah

    The lovely floral motif represents the blossoming of a young girl into womanhood as she becomes a bas mitzvah. The verse along the sides of the design is taken form Proverbs. "Many daughters have performed valiantly, but you have surpassed them all." The two Sabbath candles illuminate the scroll, with the blessing peering from behind the roses." May God make you like Sarah, Rebecca, Rachel and Leah. The phrase along the bottom completes the blessing bestowed by many fathers on their daughters upon their return from synagogue on Friday night: "May God bless you and safeguard you; may God illuminate His countenance for you and be gracious to you; may God turn His countenance to you and establish peace for you."

הדלקת נרות

יברכך ה' וישמרך
יאר ה' פניו אליך ויחנך
ישא ה' פניו אליך וישם לך שלום

A young woman becomes obligated in *mitzvos* when she reaches twelve years old and a day (*Niddah* 45b). This is a *halachah l'Moshe miSinai*, an oral tradition given to Moses at Mount Sinai. (*Rosh Responsa* 16:1, see also page 23). Marking the advent of a young woman into the realm of *mitzvah* obligation with a festive celebration is a relatively recent phenomenon.

There are divergent opinions as to the extent of the *bas mitzvah* celebration. These run the gamut from those who strictly prohibit it, to those who suggest a modest celebration, to others who contend that it is a laudable practice. Rabbinic *Responsa* on the subject are few in number, and a competent halachic authority should be consulted to determine one's practice.

☐ R' Moshe Feinstein rules that the *bas mitzvah* celebration is not a *seudas mitzvah*, but more like a birthday party with no religious significance. As such, he states that it may not be held in a synagogue, even during a time when no services are being held. He permits a private celebration in one's home, and a *kiddush* in a shul, as is done for any joyous occasion. The *bas mitzvah* girl is permitted to address the guests, but only at the *kiddush* table, and not at the *bimah*, or *lectern*, in *shul* (*Igros Moshe, O.C. Vol. I, 104, vol. II, 97 and vol. IV, 36*).

☐ Rabbi Aharon Walkin in *Z'kan Aharon,* vol. I, contends that a *bas mitzvah* celebration merely imitates confirmation celebrations of the gentiles, and violates the precepts of וּבְחֻקֹתֵיהֶם לֹא תֵלֵכוּ, *do not emulate the ways of the nations.* His objection stems also from the fact that this celebration is a recent innovation, and is rooted in the ideologies of those who deviated from traditional observance.

☐ *Seridei Aish*, however, points to the intent, as well as the actual performance, of the *bas mitzvah* celebration. Since the intent is not to emulate pagan practices of rites of passage for females, there is no violation of וּבְחֻקֹּתֵיהֶם לֹא תֵלֵכוּ (*Responsa* 93).

The concern raised by *Z'kan Aharon* that the *bas mitzvah* celebration is an innovation with questionable roots, must be viewed from a historical perspective, according to *Seridei Aish*. In earlier generations, where Torah and fear of heaven permeated almost every Jewish home, young women were infused with positive attitudes toward the Torah and its commandments. Today, however, because of the pervasive influences of secular society, it is necessary to harness our energies for the inculcation of a solid Torah education in our daughters. To that end he writes, a *bas mitzvah* celebration can be used to encourage young women to follow a life based on Torah precepts and predicated upon observance of *mitzvos*. He specifies, however, the same caveat as R' Moshe Feinstein, that *any* manner of celebration should not take place in the synagogue itself.

☐ *Ben Ish Chai,* a 19th century Sephardic authority states that although the young woman should rejoice on the day she becomes a *bas mitzvah*, it is not customary to have a festive meal. Rather, he recommends that she wear the Sabbath clothes, or don a new garment. She recites the *Shehecheyanu* blessing for the garment and should have in mind that the blessing refers also to her new status, since she is now obligated in *mitzvos*. Indeed, in his home in Baghdad all birthdays were festive occasions (*Ben Ish Chai, Re'ei* 17).

☐ Former Sephardic Chief, Rabbi Ovadiah Yosef concludes that it is permissible and indeed commendable to make a festive meal as an expression of praise to God for having become a *bas mitzvah*. Words of Torah should be part of the occasion, as well as songs of thanksgiving to God, because the celebration has religious overtones. Rabbi Yosef makes no distinction between the obligation of a young man and that of a young woman; the celebration of both is considered a *seudas mitzvah*. He cautions, however, that laws of modesty should be observed (*Yabbia Omer, vol. III, Yoreh Deah, chapter 24*).

CUSTOMS THROUGH THE AGES

✑ Introduction

hile many of the practical applications of *bar mitzvah* observance and celebration are appropriately categorized in the realm of *halachah*, Jewish law, much of the actual ritual is also dependent on one's *minhag*, custom.

The significant role that custom plays in Judaism should by no means be minimized. Adherence to one's customs is not only vital to the survival of our ancient traditions, but is also a complex issue within the *halachic* process. Clearly, individuals need to be well-versed in the customs of their ancestors and follow their paths of practice.

This section, dealing with *bar mitzvah* customs, is presented as a survey of the rich tapestry of Jewish customs and is not intended as a restatement of the definitive *halachah*. Its purpose is to examine the breadth of differing traditions within the scope of *bar mitzvah* celebration. The rich variances within our Jewish heritage is well represented by the diversity of observances and procedures of *bar mitzvah* practice around the world.

This heterogeneity is manifest not only when comparing the various cultures, but can be seen even *within* a particular tradition, where subtle differences and occasional dissonances are found. The reader is, therefore, cautioned not to use this chapter as a conclusive guide to dictate one's actual practice. A competent Rabbinical authority should always be consulted when questions arise.

Customs presented here are from various sources; researched texts, first-person accounts and observable trends. Again, none of these are definitive representations of any group, but are rather a kaleidoscopic portrait of the *bar mitzvah* celebration through the ages and around the world.

□ Many Chassidic groups follow the ruling cited in the *Shulchan Aruch* that *tefillin* are first put on when a boy becomes 13 years and one day (see *Rama, O.C.* 37:3).

When to Begin

Some of the groups included in this list are: Belz, Satmar, Alesk, Ziditchov, Komarna, Ruzhin, and Munkatch, among others.

This ruling is based on the Talmud (*Succah* 42a) which states that a *katan*, a young boy, who is sufficiently responsible to care for *tefillin*, must receive *tefillin* from his father. *Rama* (*O.C. op. cit*), quoting *Ba'al Ha'itur*, explains the Talmud to mean that only a boy of thirteen years and a day is in this category.

One reason for not allowing boys under thirteen to put on *tefillin* is cited by *Ta'amei HaMinhagim* (Vol. III; p. 12) in the name of Rebbe Shalom of Belz. It is seen as most propitious for the inspiration and supreme love that comes with the very first performance of this *mitzvah* to coincide with the first time one performs the *mitzvah* in fulfillment of the Torah commandment.

□ The Chassidim of Bobov begin *tefillin* wear one day before the *bar mitzvah*.

□ Earlier commentators, such as the *Bach* (*O.C. op. cit*) actually permit boys over twelve years old to don *tefillin*, provided they learn and understand Talmud. Some call for a six month training period (see *Migdal Oz* p. 18b).

□ Others follow the ruling of the *Mishnah Berurah* (note 12, *op. cit.*) who quotes the *Magen Avraham* (note 4, *op. cit.*) that a preparatory period of two or three months is customary.

□ The custom of many today including Chassidei Ger, Skvere, and Novominsk, is to begin one month before the *bar mitzvah* (*Aruch HaShulchan, O.C.* chap. 37; see also *Shaarei Shalom* on *Kitzur Shulchan Aruch*, Part I, p. 244). This is probably based on the Talmudic dictate that tells us to inquire about and to study the laws of Passover, beginning thirty days prior to the Festival (*Pesachim* 6a).

□ Chassidim of Lubavitch begin to put on their *tefillin* two months prior to the *bar mitzvah* (*Minhagei Chabad*).

□ In *K'hal Adas Yeshurun* boys first put on *tefillin* three months before their *bar mitzvah*.

□ In the Syrian community, *tefillin* are first donned on a Monday or Thursday before the Sabbath of one's *bar mitzvah*.

□ No set time for initial *tefillin* wear is set for Moroccan and Yemenite boys. Each one starts when he is deemed responsible enough to be educated properly. While many of them begin a few months before their *bar mitzvah*, even a boy as young as ten or eleven could conceivably wear *tefillin* (see Rabbi Y. Kapach, *Halichot Teiman*, 1960 p. 182; also *Yellin, Yehoshua, Zichronos l'Bar Yerushalayim*, 5684).

□ Some *bar mitzvah* boys in Judeo-Spanish communities begin their *tefillin* training six months prior to the *bar mitzvah* (*Keter Shem Tob*, R' Shemtob Gaguine I 13, 24). Others start as early as twelve and one day (*A Treasury of Sephardic Laws and Customs*, Dobrinsky, Herbert C., New York 1986).

□ Boys of Spanish-Portuguese heritage have very little training before their *bar mitzvah*, usually not more than a few weeks.

Among those who do put on *tefillin* before *bar mitzvah*, are some who do it with a *brachah*, and others without. *Zera Emes* (Part III, chap. 5) and *Even Sheseyah* (chap. 14),

Brachah Before Bar Mitzvah

among others, rule that a *brachah* should be recited. *Tzofnas Pa'aneach* opines that no *brachah* should be said. (See also *Mishnah Berurah* chap. 658; *Shaarei Tzion* note 36 for a fuller discussion of this topic).

□ While some boys in the Sephardic communities do not recite a *brachah* before *bar mitzvah*, most of them do.

□ The prevailing custom in Chabad circles is not to make a *brachah* for the first month. When the child is more accustomed to wearing his *tefillin* properly, he begins reciting a *brachah* (*Minhagei Chabad* p. 4).

❀ ❀ ❀

□ Among those who do not put on *tefillin* before the *bar mitzvah*, there are differing customs as to whether *tefillin* should be donned earlier than the *bar mitzvah* day if it falls out on a Sabbath or Festival (when *tefillin* are never worn).

□ Most Chassidic groups do put on *tefillin* before the Sabbath or Festivals, even if the *bar mitzvah* is on Chol Hamoed. A *brachah* is usually recited. The Chassidim of Dinev do not make a *brachah* prior to the *bar mitzvah* (see *Bnei Yissoschor*).

☐ The Chassidim of Munkatch wait until after the Sabbath (Sunday morning) or Festivals to put on *tefillin* .[1]

The custom among the Sephardic communities is to follow the ruling of the *Shulchan Aruch* (O.C. 25:5) that only one *brachah* is recited

How Many Berachos?

for the *shel yad* and the *shel rosh* — „בָּרוּךְ. . .לְהָנִיחַ תְּפִילִין"

☐ The one possible exception to this practice amongst the Sephardim is within Moroccan circles. The first and only time a Moroccan boy says two *brachos* (בָּרוּךְ. . . עַל מִצְוַת תְּפִילִין before tightening the *shel rosh*) is on the day of his *bar mitzvah*. He is instructed to intentionally speak after donning the *shel yad* in order to necessitate the recital of the *brachah* for the *shel rosh*. Thereafter, he only says one *brachah* , and is told never to speak again between putting on the *shel yad* and the *shel rosh* (*Miminhagei Yahadut Morocco, R' Shalom Danino*, p. 270).

☐ All other communities (Ashkenaz etc.) follow the ruling of the *Rama* (O.C. 25:5), and say two *brachos* (see also *Ba'er Heitev* and *Shaarei Teshuvah ibid.*).

Generally speaking, most Sephardim sit while donning the *shel yad* and stand for the *shel rosh*. Most Ashkenazim stand while putting on

Sitting or Standing

both. [See *Rama, O.C.* 25:11]. There are, however, exceptions in practice. *Magen Avraham* (*ibid.* note 20) distinguishes between reciting the *brachah* and putting on the *tefillin* . The *brachah* and the tightening of the *shel yad* are done standing, the *shel yad* is wound on the arm while one is seated, and the *shel rosh* is put on while standing. The Chassidim of Munkatch, Alesk and Komarna follow this view. According to the *Zohar* and the *Arizal* , even the *brachah* is said while one is sitting (*Shalmei Tzibbur* p. 8a).[2]

---

1. R' Yitzchak Isaac Handler of Brooklyn, New York recalls that his *bar mitzvah* was on the second day of Passover in 1935 in Munkatch. The first time he put on *tefillin* was seven days later — the day after Passover! The Rebbe, ז"ל supervised and assisted him with his *tefillin*, while reminding him of the overwhelming significance of never discussing secular matters with his *tefillin* on.

2. The Klausenberger Rebbe, שליט"א has an interesting custom of putting on the *shel yad* while he is in a leaning position (i.e. as if he were partially standing and partially sitting). A source for this practice might be the *Maharsham* (notes on *Shulchan Aruch*, chap. 25 in *Orchas Chaim*).

The direction in which one winds the *retzuah* straps on his arm is also dependent on his custom. Here the practice usually follows the

Direction of Winding

nusach that one uses when he prays. ☐ Those who pray *nusach* Sephard wind the *retzuah* away from the body, as do Chassidei Lubavitch. Those who pray *nusach* Ashkenaz tie the *retzuah* toward the body. Here, too, variations do exist, so an inquiry should be made if any doubt arises as to which custom one should follow.

CUSTOMS

As discussed earlier, there are actually two types of *tefillin* — the *tefillin* of *Rashi* and the *tefillin* of *Rabbeinu Tam* (see pp. 74).

Tefillin of Rabbeinu Tam

The universal custom is to wear the *tefillin* of *Rashi* and recite the *brachos* (or *brachah*) on those *tefillin* (*Shulchan Aruch, O.C. 34:1*).

☐ There are those who also put on the *tefillin* of *Rabbeinu Tam* (without a *brachah*). Only those who are very exacting in the performance of all the *mitzvos*, however, should follow this practice (*ibid. 34:3; see also Ba'er Heitev, Shaarei Teshuvah, Mishnah Berurah loc. cit.*).

☐ Although there are those who remove the *Rashi tefillin* after *kedushah* during the *chazzan's* repetition of *Shemoneh Esrei*, many do not consider this to be correct practice (*M.B. 34:14*). The *tefillin* of *Rabbeinu Tam* should ideally be put on after *aleinu*, at the end of *Shacharis*.

☐ On Rosh Chodesh, when the *tefillin* are removed prior to *Mussaf*, those who wear the *tefillin* of *Rabbeinu Tam* should don them either after *Mussaf* or prior to the prayer *Uvo L'Tzion* (*Pri Megadim*, quoted by *M.B. 25:60*).

☐ Those who wear *tefillin* on Chol Hamoed, do not wear the *tefillin* of *Rabbeinu Tam* on those days (*ibid.*).

☐ Even among those who do put on *tefillin* before the *bar mitzvah*, the *tefillin* of *Rabbeinu Tam* are not put on until after the *bar mitzvah*.

☐ Chabad Chassidim currently put on *Rabbeinu Tam's tefillin* immediately after *bar mitzvah*. Their custom had been to wait until the eighteenth birthday, but that is no longer the case.

☐ Chassidei Ger, Bobov, Satmar and Sanz wait until they are married before they put on the *tefillin* of *Rabbeinu Tam*. The custom of Belz and others is to wait until one year after marriage to put on the *tefillin* of *Rabbeinu Tam*.

Numbers that Soar
Reb Osher Zelig Margolis was very close to the late Satmar Rav, Rabbi Yoel Teitelbaum, צ"ל, in Eretz Yisrael in 1946. When the Rav decided to leave Eretz Yisrael for America, Reb Osher Zelig asked him, "Now that you're leaving, to whom can I give a kvittel (a written request to pray on one's behalf)?"
The Rav replied. "Go into one of the shtieblach, where people come in to daven. When you see a man rolling up his sleeve to put on tefillin — he doesn't have to have a beard — and there are concentration camp numbers on his arm, you know you can give him a kvittel."

מנהגי
CUTOM
העולם

□ There was, at one time, a custom for those who wore the *tefillin* of *Rabbeinu Tam*, to wear the two pairs simultaneously (*Shulchan Aruch*, *O.C.* 34:2; also *Mishnah Berurah* and *Be'ur Halachah ibid.*). Today, only a few select scholars in Sephardic communities still practice this tradition (see *Eretz Chaim*, *R' Chaim Sitton* 34:2-3), including some from Tangier and other Moroccan cities (see *Kehillat Sefrou*, *R' David Ovadia*, III 265:5). It is because of this custom that the *tefillin* of Sephardim are usually smaller than those of Ashkenazim — in order to accommodate simultaneous wear.[1]

□ It is the custom of many not to wear *tefillin* on Chol Hamoed, since it is similar to the Sabbath and Festivals (*Shulchan Aruch*, *O.C.* 31:2).

Chol Hamoed

□ Others such as *K'hal Adas Yeshurun* follow *Rama (ibid.)* and wear *tefillin* on Chol Hamoed. Among this group, most do not recite a *brachah*, although some do (see *Taz* and *M. B. ibid.* note 8).

□ While Sephardim and most Chassidic groups do not wear *tefillin* on Chol Hamoed, the custom of Sanz is for unmarried men to wear *tefillin* on Chol Hamoed. Unmarried men who follow Bobov traditions also don *tefillin* on Chol Hamoed, but only until the age of eighteen.

□ Satmar practice has no uniformity regarding this. While no married men wear *tefillin* on Chol Hamoed, some unmarrieds do and some do not.

□ Those who wear *tefillin* on Chol Hamoed should do so with the following conditions in mind: "If I am required to wear *tefillin* on Chol Hamoed, I wish to fulfill this *mitzvah*; if not, I am not wearing them in order to fulfill a *mitzvah*" (*M. B. ibid.*).

Procedures for appropriate removal of the *tefillin* have been previously discussed (see p. 82). While some follow the ruling of

Removing the Tefillin

the *Shulchan Aruch (O.C.* 25:13) and take off the *tefillin* after the "Kedushah" portion of *Uvo L'Tzion*, most wait until after the final *Kaddish (Rama ibid.)*.

□ *Ba'al Ha'itur* reports that in the post-Talmudic era of the Geonim, when *tefillin* were worn all day, the *tefillin* would be removed prior to

---

1. The Sanzer Rav, זצ״ל had the custom of wearing the *tefillin* of *Rashi* and *Rabbeinu Tam* simultaneously, *before davening!* During davening he wore only the *tefillin* of *Rashi*.

after-*Minchah* meal on the Sabbath. The *bar mitzvah* boy himself was required to invite everyone personally to the *seudah* by visiting them only one hour before the meal (*see* account of R' Yospe on p. 121)!

☐ The poorer people of Glogau, Germany in 1688 were accustomed to invite 30 people (including servants) to a *bar mitzvah seudah*. Families of slightly greater means invited 40 people, while richer folk had no limit (*Geschiechte der Judean in Schlesien, Breslau 1907, ff. Anhang* VII, p. 89).

☐ The accounts of the customs of the Fuerth community in 1728 are even more descriptive. The size of the invitation list was totally dependant on one's income and ranged between 10 and 24 people. Except for blood relatives and first cousins, women were not invited. The smaller the affair, the more laudatory it was considered. Everyone was served a measure of wine and unlimited beer. Those of the lower economic strata could serve only turkey (*tarnegoles Hodu*) and fish if the cost per portion was less than 15 *kreuitzer*. The next highest income group was allowed to serve two turkeys, sardines and lox — up to 20 *kreuitzer*. There was no limit on the consumption of wine. Those who were more affluent could serve three turkeys and fish (*Das Tekunnos Buechlein*, (1728) *Frankfort und Prag,* 1754 pp. 124 and 126).

☐ The guidelines for the city of Runkel in 1749 displayed noteworthy sensitivity. They dictated that in order to avoid potential jealousy and ill-will only relatives living within city limits could be invited. Non-relatives, however, could be invited even if they lived far away.

☐ Besides guests from "out-of-town," members of the Prague community in 1767 could invite only 10 people, plus the *bar mitzvah* boy, his father, and his friends. No exceptions were permitted. The only women invited were close relatives.

A great emphasis was placed on the mood of the celebration. No musical or comedy presentations were permitted and the menu was considerably sparce. Only the one who led the *bircas hamazon*, grace after meals, was permitted to have a full cup of wine and no coffee was allowed!

☐ The Jewish communities in 1783 Italy permitted themselves just 36 guests and served either fish or meat — not both.

✼ ✼ ✼

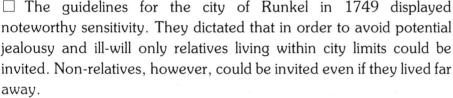

Joyful Beginnings
The first mitzvah that a bar mitzvah boy performs is that of being b'simchah, in happiness. When nightfall begins and he officially becomes a bar mitzvah, he rejoices that the privilege of accepting the obligation to perform all mitzvos is upon him. This emotion is a fulfillment of the Biblical commandment requiring one to serve God with complete joy and a good heart.
— Chasam Sofer, Vayechi

CUSTOMS

Nowadays, expenditures for *bar mitzvah* celebrations vary greatly. The absence of effective central authority in most Jewish communities allows each family to plan celebrations in any fashion it wishes.

☐ There are some attempts, however, especially among Chassidic groups, to limit the extravagance of *simchah* celebrations. Many of these groups have limited the number of guests and the menus of these occasions.

☐ Agudath Israel of America recently issued guidelines for such expenditure limitations for their member synagogues. They considered this action to be part of a ". . .broad effort at self-improvement in a wide range of areas to raise the quality of Jewish life to a new and higher plane."

Their recommendations include:

    a: *Kiddush* for a *yahrzeit:* Cake and drinks only.

    b: *Kiddush* on the birth of a daughter, or other *Seudas Hoda'ah* (expression of gratitude to the Almighty): One additional item may be served, such as fish or a hot dish.

    c: *Kiddush* for a *bar mitzvah* or *aufruf:* Two additional items may be served, for example, fish plus a hot dish.

    d: The *simchah* should be arranged only in the shul itself or its own reception facility.

Coalition, March 1991

Sephardic Celebration

In the Syrian community, the celebration for a *bar mitzvah* boy is divided into two parts. The first part takes place on the Monday or Thursday morning prior to the *bar mitzvah Sabbath*, when he puts on *tefillin* for the first time and is called to the Torah. A joyous breakfast feast usually follows the synagogue service and an all-day "open-house" is often held afterwards.

The Sabbath service is traditionally followed by a large *kiddush*, known as a *sabt*. Special *pizmonim*, songs, are sung at the *sabt* and *besamim*, spices, are distributed. The guests recite the blessing for the spices and smell the fragrances.

☐ Many Moroccan families still follow the ancient custom of inviting a barber to the home on the night before the *bar mitzvah*. The *bar mitzvah* boy and his father are given haircuts, which are accompanied by melodious singing of special tunes for the occasion (*Danino, Miminhagei Yahadut Morocco*, p. 269-270).

The *bar mitzvah* boy is accompanied to the synagogue the next morning by family members holding lit candles. He is escorted home the same way.

☐ Moroccan families of means have a beautiful custom of arranging a simultaneous *bar mitzvah* celebration for two orphans or poor children, in exactly the same fashion as that of their own child.[1]

☐ Sephardic boys put on a *talis* when they become *bar mitzvah*. The *talis* is thereafter donned every morning at Shacharis, the morning prayers. Some recite the *shehecheyanu* blessing the first time they put on the *talis*.

⤐ The Celebration: Historical Accounts

To portray typical *bar mitzvah* celebrations of years ago, we present three accounts:

The following narrative is from the *Sefer Haminhagim* (Book of Customs) of R' Yospe HaLevi (1604-1678), the sexton of the **Germany** Congregation of Worms, Germany. He describes the *bar mitzvah* celebration which took place in Worms in the year 1617.

. . .On the Sabbath following the day that a boy reaches the age of 13 years and one day, most boys read the sidrah, Torah portion, for the congregation. The prayer before the reading, V'Ya'azor V'Yagen. . . , [May He assist and shield,. . .] is begun in a melodious tune.

Those youngsters with especially sweet voices and familiarity with prayer lead the congregation in any or all of the Sabbath tefilos, prayers.

Those who do not possess the necessary skills to read aloud from the Torah, are nevertheless called up to the Torah for an aliyah. At that time, two Mi Sheberach's (blessings for the person called up to the Torah) are recited. In the second, the bar mitzvah boy states his pledge to donate a measure of oil to help illuminate the synagogue.

Upon the onset of the Sabbath, the father of the bar mitzvah boy provides beautiful, new clothes for his son to wear that day.

One hour prior to the Minchah service on the Sabbath afternoon, the bar mitzvah boy himself, not the sexton, personally visits the

---

1. A similar custom was practiced by many American families in the 1980's. "Twinning," as it was called, involved the symbolic practice of choosing a Russian boy who, was unable to celebrate his *bar mitzvah* behind The Iron Curtain. The boy's name usually appeared on the invitation together with the name of the "real" *bar mitzvah* boy.

CUTOM

homes of his relatives and friends, and invites them to join him for *shalosh seudos*, the traditional third Sabbath meal. This meal is especially designated as the "Bar Mitzvah Seudah," at which time he delivers a Torah discourse and also leads the assembled in Bircas Hamazon, Grace after Meals.

The Jews of Morocco celebrate a *bar mitzvah* somewhat differently. The following account, taken from an 1839 report in the German newspaper *Allgemeine Zeitung des Judenthums*, sheds light on their rich culture and traditions.

Morocco

The bar mitzvah preparations of a Moroccan boy begin when he reaches 12 years and one day. At that time, the boy begins studying a Talmudic discourse with his father or rabbi. The discourse is usually taken from tractates Chullin, Menachos, or Kesubos, and their accompanying commentaries — Rashi, Tosafos, Maharsha etc. The depth of the discourse varies according to the capacities and development of the boy. The discourse is reviewed every evening until the boy has mastered every aspect of it and knows it by heart.

At the end of the year, the boy submits to a rigorous examination by the local scholars. Afterwards, neighborhood rabbis, community leaders, friends and relatives are invited to participate in a special meal, which is always held on a Wednesday before the bar mitzvah.

On Thursday morning, Shacharis, [the morning prayers], is recited in the boy's home. The chief rabbi assists the boy in donning the shel yad tefillin on his arm and then his father helps him place the shel rosh on his head. Choral presentations accompany this ceremony. The bar mitzvah boy purchases the privilege of designating which people receive the honors of the Torah reading. A Kohen is called first — then a Levi — followed by the bar mitzvah boy. (On Rosh Chodesh the bar mitzvah boy receives the fourth (and final) aliyah.

A somber mood then permeates the room as the bar mitzvah boy commences his long awaited Torah discourse. This takes place between the recital of ashrei and uva l'tzion. The women assembled there would often cry, especially because the discourse was held in Arabic, which they could understand. Scholars in attendance would engage the boy in deeper discussions on the subject matter. Upon his conclusion, the boy would revel in the unified chants of the gathering

"May you be strong and blessed to enhance the Torah and beautify it!"

The bar mitzvah boy descends from the podium and greets all the men with one hand outstretched and the other holding his tefillin pouch. He then approaches the women guests. Many, including his parents, present him with gifts which he subsequently gives to his teacher.

The guests leave after breakfast and return in the evening for more festivities. The boy reads the haftarah on the following Sabbath. The congregants honor the bar mitzvah boy by singing a song by R' Dovid ben Chassin, as he ascends to the Torah.

North Africa

Another *bar mitzvah* celebration in North Africa is described in a German book entitled, "Acht Jahre in Asien und Afrika von 1846 bis 1855," Hannover 1858 pp. 275-276.[1] Here is the account:

Several weeks before a boy reaches 13, the Rabbi prepares a drashah, Torah discourse, for him. On the Sabbath prior to the bar mitzvah, which is called "tefillin," the boy's relatives gather for a feast that lasts until Sunday morning.

On Sunday afternoon, the women, dressed in their finery, visit the friends of the family in their homes and the classmates in their school to invite them to a party. When the guests are assembled, a barber is brought in to cut the hair of the bar mitzvah boy and his friends. All who participate donate money towards this expense.[2]

Following the haircut, a joyous celebration ensues, which lasts until morning!

The Chacham, [Rabbi] and the teacher of the bar mitzvah boy both come to the home of the bar mitzvah boy on Monday morning. They adorn him with his talis and tefillin and lead him and his friends on the road to the synagogue. The journey is enhanced by singing and glowing candlelight.

The synagogue is decorated in honor of this most special occasion.

During the Torah reading for that particular Monday morning, the three aliyos, honor of being called to the Torah, are given to the

---

1. This book has since been translated into Hebrew by David Gordon under the title *"Massei Yisrael."*

2. This ceremony is also practiced by the Syrian community prior to a wedding. The marriage celebration is said to begin with the groom's haircut, which is enhanced by specifically designated songs and dances in his presence.

CUSTOMS

father of the bar mitzvah boy, a family member and the bar mitzvah boy himself. [1]

The Chacham then blesses the bar mitzvah boy prior to his discourse. The boy's father and other relatives give charity to poor people.

When the program in the synagogue has been completed, all the congregants congratulate the boy and accompany him homeward to a festive meal.

The bar mitzvah boy, still wearing his talis and tefillin, and accompanied by his friends, thereupon visits the homes of his female blood relatives. There, each woman is given the honor of removing a tefillin strap from the boy's arm. A monetary gift is usually given by those honored.

When all the visits have been completed, the boy goes home, puts away his talis and tefillin, and embarks on an outing with his friends . . . In the evening, friends and relatives again gather in the home of the bar mitzvah boy for a final, all-night celebration.

⇜ Siyum

In recent years, bar mitzvah boys have been encouraged to make a siyum in honor of their bar mitzvahs.

In many circles, the bar mitzvah boy will study a tractate of Talmud or a complete order of Mishnah and complete the project in time for him to celebrate the siyum at his bar mitzvah seudah. Some especially gifted bar mitzvah boys undertake to learn all six orders of the Mishnah!

⇜ Tachanun

There are differing customs regarding whether to recite tachanun in the synagogue if a bar mitzvah boy is present in the congregation on the day of his bar mitzvah. (Of course, this refers only to a weekday morning since tachanun is never said on the Sabbath.)

☐ Among Chassidic circles, no clear pattern emerges. Many Chassidim do not say tachanun that morning, but Chassidei Bobov,

---

1. This sequence is intentional since a son is not called to the Torah immediately after his father because of ayin hora, fear of an evil eye (see Shulchan Aruch, Orach Chaim 141:6; also Shaarei Ephraim 1:30-33).

Satmar, and Ger, among others, do (see *Tzitz Eliezer*, vol. II, chap. 17).

☐ The Munkatcher Rebbe was very diligent about reciting *tachanun* — even on the *yahrzeit* of his great Rabbinic ancestors (the *Shem MiShmuel* and the *Bnei Yissoschor*). When a boy celebrated his *bar mitzvah*, however, he omitted *tachanun*. (*Darkei Chaim V'Shalom* §192) [1]

☐ Sephardim generally follow the custom of not saying *tachanun* on the day of a boy's *bar mitzvah* if he is present in the congregation (*Yabbia Omer*, vol. IV, chap. 14).

◄§ Torah Reading

☐ When a boy reaches his *bar mitzvah* age, he is permitted to *lain*, read the Torah aloud for the congregation. Although one must have reached his physical maturity as well, in order to discharge the congregation's obligation, there is no need for him to prove this. Once he becomes thirteen, we may assume that he is physically mature — thus allowing him to *lain* (*M.B.* 282:13).

☐ Many boys study the entire *sidrah*, Torah portion, and read it aloud on the Sabbath of their *bar mitzvah*; others read only the *maftir* portion, the final few verses, and the *haftarah*.

☐ Generally speaking, in the environs of the Yeshivos of Lithuania and Poland, *bar mitzvah* boys did not read from the Torah. In some places, it was even frowned upon as being a non-scholarly endeavor for a yeshivah student.

☐ A *bar mitzvah* boy does not *lain Parshas Zachor*, which is read on the Sabbath before *Purim*. This is because this reading, recalling the evil deeds of *Amalek*, may be Scriptural in origin, thus requiring that it be read by a full-fledged, physically mature adult, in order to discharge the congregation of its obligation.

---

1. This custom is followed on the first day that one puts on *tefillin*, even if his actual *bar mitzvah* day was earlier (e.g. if his *bar mitzvah* day was on the *Sabbath*, a Festival, or Chol Hamoed).

No Leftovers
A bar mitzvah celebration was once graced with the presence of the great Rebbe of Belz, R' Aharon זצ"ל. The Rebbe instructed the bar mitzvah boy to lead those assembled in the bircas hamazon, Grace After Meals. When the bentching was over, the Rebbe noticed that the boy had drunk only most of the wine in the cup — correctly following the minimum requirement of the law (O.C. 190). R' Aharon protested, requesting that the boy finish all the wine. Afterwards the Rebbe explained his insistence: "During the holiday of Chanukah, we celebrate the incredible miracle that God performed for us — giving us pure, clean oil to light the menorah in the Bais Hamikdash which implausibly lasted eight days instead of one. But the commentator Pnei Yehoshua (on Tractate Shabbos 21b) wonders why this miracle was even necessary, since for a tzibbur, a public offering of people, one may even use unclean oil, if none other is available (see Pesachim 77a)? He answers that we can understand from this that Hashem wanted to inaugurate this great mitzvah of lighting the menorah in the most complete and splendid way possible — not with just a minimum requirement. "Similarly," explained the Rebbe, "when the bar mitzvah boy, for the very first time can lead us in this great mitzvah of birchas hamazon, he too should perform it in the most complete and beautiful way possible.

⇜ Prayer

Since the concept of *shliach tzibbur* (*"chazzan"*), is of Rabbinic origin, a *bar mitzvah* boy may lead the congregation in prayer, even without confirmation of his physical maturity (*Levush, O.C.* chap. 53, note 10; also *Magen Avraham, O.C.* loc. cit. note 10. See also *M.B.* 53:25).

⇜ Grace After Meals

☐ Some have the custom of asking the *bar mitzvah* boy to lead the *Bircas Hamazon*, Grace after Meals, at the *seudah* given in his honor (*Aruch HaShulchan* 199:4). While no one objects to this practice, many choose to honor someone else (a grandfather or a rabbi) with this distinction.

☐ The Belzer Rebbe took special care to honor a *bar mitzvah* boy with the Grace after Meals if his birthday was on the Sabbath. Since no *tefillin* are worn that day, the boy's role in leading the *bentching* served as the proclamation that he is now a halachic adult. A *minyan*, ten adult males, should be present at that time.

⇜ *Shehecheyanu*

Because it is questionable of whether the *shehecheyanu* blessing should be recited when one first puts on *tefillin*, it may be advisable for the *bar mitzvah* boy to wear a new suit at the same time. The *shehecheyanu* blessing then serves as an expression of gratitude for both events (*M.B.* 22:22 and *Be'ur Halachah* loc. cit.). This, of course, could not apply to those whose custom it is to begin wearing *tefillin* before one's *bar mitzvah*, since at that time he is not obligated to perform the *mitzvah* (see pp. 110).

☐ Others connect the *shehecheyanu* blessing, not to the wearing of *tefillin*, but to his newly acquired obligation to perform *mitzvos* (see *Chasan Sofer, O.C.* 55). Still others do not agree that this obligation would require a *shehecheyanu* blessing (*Igros Moshe, Yoreh Deah* vol. III, chap. 14, note 4).

☐ Most Sephardic boys recite the *shehecheyanu* when they begin wearing a *Talis* after the *bar mitzvah*.

PROFILES and PERSONALITIES

Elisha — Man of Wings

    The artplate on the following page depicts the story of Elisha — Man of Wings (see page 135). The micrographic border around the artwork is formed from the four parshiyos, Torah portions, found in the tefillin worn by man. The tefillin hovering above Elisha are the tefillin that are worn, as it were, by God. These contain verses of praise to God's nation, the Jewish people (Berachos 6a).

◆§ An Excused Lateness

I suppose Naftali was no different than any other *bar mitzvah* boy. Proud. Excited. Nervous, of course. But his father's request did not seem unusual in any way. The day would soon be over and the *seudah*, festive meal, would begin shortly. It made sense for him to be at the hall a bit early — before the guests begin to arrive. Living within a short walk of the hall was a convenient benefit and the rest of his family would follow within a few minutes.

And so it was. Naftali's family, as expected, made their way to the *simchah* hall, but were met with quite a surprise when they arrived. The guests were indeed filing in, but Naftali was nowhere to be found! Guests were queried, rooms were searched — but no clues surfaced.

Puzzling as the situation was, however, panic did not really settle in. After all, times long ago were not like they are now. Streets were safer, criminal activity was infrequent, and people traveled about with a relatively carefree attitude. So, while most people wondered about Naftali's whereabouts, few of them actually worried. "He'll show up soon," they reasoned.

The guests were all seated and the soup was cooling off when a frenzied, but proud Naftali appeared on the scene. A curious throng soon surrounded the *bar mitzvah* boy to hear the explanation for his lateness. The captive audience heard him tell the following tale:

"I can only tell you what I was told. How you understand it, is up to you. It seems that the news began to circulate beyond the heavenly gates that the great sage, Rabbi Shimon bar Yochai and his learned

profiles and personalities

son, were planning to reveal incredible Torah insights from the cave in which they were hiding for years.

When our father, Abraham, heard the report, he made immediate plans to attend this most inspirational event. Knowing full well that this rare occasion would surely be appreciated by others, he related the news to his son Isaac, who, of course, decided immediately to come. Isaac naturally told his son Jacob about the inspirational secrets of Torah that were certain to emanate from the minds of those sages and Jacob invited Joseph to join his father, grandfather and great-grandfather at this unusual lecture.

By the time the heavenly party was prepared to embark to R' Shimon's cave, the illustrious travelers also included Moses, Aaron and King David. The greatest leaders in Jewish history would soon assemble in one place, to bask in the radiance of Hashem's Torah.

They were not disappointed. For hours and hours the Torah mystique filled the musty cavern that R' Shimon was forced to call "home". And when the discussion concluded and the day came to a close, R' Shimon turned to his illustrious guests and asked one small favor of them. "It is so rare that we see anyone in this cave, certainly not such worthy guests as you. And naturally my son and I never get a chance to daven with a minyan of ten people. How glorious it would be to be able to pray together and exalt the greatness of God!"

Willing as they all were, though, a quick count revealed the undeniable fact that this great gathering still lacked one person. A group of nine, no matter how pious and erudite, could still not constitute a minyan.

"Let's look outside for a tenth Jew to join us in prayer," someone suggested.

It was just then that I was walking by and was able to answer 'Yes' when I was asked if I was bar mitzvah. As you might expect, it was a minchah I'll never forget."

❧ ❧ ❧

This story never actually took place. But it *could* have. The facts are incidental to the imposing message this story teaches us.

The greatest Jews who ever lived can gather together. Abraham, Moses, King David and six other colleagues can desire to pray together. But without Naftali, just thirteen years old, the glory of Hashem's kingdom cannot be told. *Kadosh, kadosh, kadosh* cannot be uttered and the words of *kaddish* cannot be recited. Every Jew, regardless of age or scholarship, is a vital link in the majestic service of prayer.

created and related by: Rabbi Meshulim Feish Ginsberg
Brooklyn, New York

◆§ The *Tefillin* of the *Or HaChaim*

It is not easy to understand. Not easy to imagine. And yet we know that it was so. The *kedushah*, level of holiness, of our Sages and previous great Rabbinic leaders was so awesome, that many of them actually wore their *tefillin* for all or most of the day.

One such *gaon* was *Rabbeinu* Chaim ibn Attar, better known as the *"Or HaChaim Hakadosh"* (1696-1743). Constant streams of ardent followers of the *tzaddik* would frequent his home and study, in the hope of benefiting from his great wisdom. But the mere sight of the *Or HaChaim*, absorbed in his Torah and adorned in his *tefillin*, was usually sufficient to leave an everlasting impression on all.

When the Sage had already reached an advanced age and was nearing death, his wife expressed concern about her future. "After you leave this world I will be left alone and penniless," she cried. "Who will support me? How will I survive?" she wailed. *Rabbeinu* Chaim heard the pleas of his distraught wife and comforted her with the words of the prophet Jeremiah, "Still your voice from crying and your eyes from tears. Look at the *tefillin* on my head and arm — they will support you. They will take care of your needs."

"After my death," he continued, "a man of great means will approach you and offer 300 gold coins for these *tefillin* — enough to sustain you forever. You will sell the *tefillin* to this man — but one firm condition must accompany the transaction. You are to instruct him to uphold the precious sanctity of these *tefillin* and to never, *ever*, speak of mundane or unspiritual matters while wearing them."

And so it was. A short while after the passing of the "Or HaChaim," a wealthy Jew purchased the *tefillin* and heard the words of caution that came along with them, . . ."and never speak while wearing these *tefillin*."

With total reverence and unyielding resolve, the gentleman treasured his priceless acquisition, fully accepting the huge responsibility it carried. Indeed, upon arriving in his home, he softly cradled the *tefillin* in his arms and with guarded anticipation proudly donned

PROFILES and PERSONALITIES מידות

them for the very first time. Never before had he felt such sanctity and grace. Never before had he *ever* experienced such elevation in spirit — such pride and dignity. Never before had his *tefillos*, (prayers), ever emanated such glory and splendor while making their heavenly ascent. The transformation was remarkable. The power of the *tefillin* was limitless.

In order to acquire this wealth, of course, this man had amassed a large network of businesses and investment opportunities. Clearly unable to keep track of this multi-faceted commercial empire alone, he hired several associates whose job it was to report daily to him on the current status of each operation.

One day he was visited by one of his colleagues seeking his expert counsel on an impending business dilemma. Distracted by the magnitude of the decision, he forgot that he was wearing THE TEFILLIN while he discussed this mundane matter.

When he subsequently returned to pray, the aura of *kedushah*, holiness, had vanished. Like the dimmed glow of the sun during a total eclipse, the light of inspiration had been extinguished. An empty void solemnly lingered over the broken man. The magic was gone.

With swift determination amid a desperate hope, he removed the *tefillin* and ran to the local *sofer*, scribe, to diagnose the malady. But to his utter horror, the expertise of a specialist was totally unnecessary. When the *batim* creaked open, releasing the parchments from their home, the diagnosis became immediately apparent. The *parshiyos* were blank! All the letters had disappeared!

Despondent and racked with grief, the man's heart sank. The words of the *Or HaChaim Hakadosh* rang loudly and convincingly, *"Never, ever, speak of unspiritual matters while wearing the tefillin."* A painful lesson had been learned.

Elisha — Man of Wings

PROFILES **AND** **PERSONALITIES** **מידות**

One of the evil decrees that the Roman government proclaimed against the Jews was a prohibition against wearing *tefillin*. "Any Jew found wearing *tefillin* would have his brains pierced through," they warned.

There lived a *tzaddik*, however, named Elisha, who dared to defy the enemy. Risking his life, Elisha would put on *tefillin* and even walk in the street while wearing them.

One day a Roman officer observed Elisha walking in the street and noticed the *tefillin* on his head! When Elisha perceived that he was in imminent danger, he began to flee. The officer took up the pursuit immediately and eventually caught up with him.

Seconds before the capture, Elisha quickly removed the *tefillin* and clutched them in his hand.

"What are you holding?" demanded the commander.

"The wings of a dove," replied Elisha. He stretched out his hand and, behold, there appeared — miraculously — the wings of a dove! Thereafter he was known as *Elisha — Ba'al K'nofayim* — Man of Wings.

※ ※ ※

The reason he chose the wings of a dove rather than any other bird is because the People of Israel is likened to a dove. Just as a dove is protected by its wings so too is Israel, protected by its *mitzvos* (*Shabbos* 49a).

The explanation is as follows: all birds use both wings to fly. When they tire, they rest on a rock. But the dove, when tired, rests on one wing and flies with the other. So too, Israel. Even when driven from one country, it always finds refuge in another country (*Tosafos* from *Midrash Rabbah, Lech Lecha* 39).

※ ※ ※

The *Chasam Sofer* (*Shabbos* 49a) asks two intriguing questions about this inspirational tale.

1) Why did Elisha remove the *tefillin*? We know that *mitzvos* have the capacity to save and protect us?

2) The Talmud relates that only someone with a *guf naki*, clean

body, like Elisha should put on *tefillin*. What in the narrative teaches us that Elisha had a *guf naki*?

He answers that Elisha felt that he *had* to remove the *tefillin* — because he knew he was about to tell a lie. Having a truly *clean body* means being unable to lie with your *tefillin* on, even to save your life.

Something to Live For

There was very little that distinguished Markstadt from other concentration camps. Thousands entered — few left. Living conditions did not vary much from other waiting rooms of death. A bowl of brown water passed for soup, and even that was hard to come by. Sleep was rare and work was grueling. Hygiene was non-existent.

Within Markstadt, however, some of the prisoners were markedly different from others. One such group was unique by virtue of its incredible dedication to the *mitzvah* of *tefillin*. Despite airtight security and unimaginable risks, one man had dared to smuggle in a pair of *tefillin*. His name was R' Binyamin Schachner, ע"ה.

Born in Sannok, a small Galician town, R' Binyamin had already suffered through other camps before his transfer to Markstadt. So upon his arrival, when he was asked if he was adept at carpentry, he knew to answer yes without hesitation. In truth, R' Binyamin barely knew at which end to hold a hammer, but expertise in a trade often meant the difference between survival and extinction.

It was in the carpentry shop that R' Binyamin found a safe hiding place for the precious *tefillin*. Loosening a wood plank in the wall, he carefully hid the *tefillin* each day after he and his friends risked their lives in performing the *mitzvah* they cherished.

Each day the perils they faced mounted, until one day the situation reached a dizzying climax. The SS guard, who was known as Jonas, entered the factory and noticed a board hanging loosely on the wall. Before the terror-filled eyes of the onlooking heroes, Jonas ripped the plank off the wall, reached in, and held the evidence in his hand.

"Whose are these?" he bellowed menacingly, staring at the Jews who refused to meet his eyes.

"I will ask once more," he warned. "If there is no answer I will hold everyone here responsible for this forbidden possession."

It was R' Binyamin who broke the silence. "They belonged to a young boy who was a prisoner here," he lied. He has since died."

But Jonas knew better. "Perhaps that is so," he said, "but your knowledge of their existence here makes *you* equally responsible!"

With that, R' Binyamin was escorted out of the shop, en route to face the brutal beatings they called *tzeinschmidt*. Few people lived to endure the entire assault and after just a few blows R' Binyamin had already suffered significant hearing damage and a substantial loss of blood.

Meanwhile, inside the shop, his inmates moved swiftly. The knew that in a matter of moments R' Binyamin's sacred life could be over. Desperate and beyond serious options, they approached the barracks' capo (Jewish guard loyal to the Nazis) to plead R' Binyamin's case. Boruch was known to be cruel, but not totally without compassion. Miraculously, their cries were heard. Boruch agreed to approach Jonas to plead R' Binyamin's case.

After a short, but agonizing wait, the frail, battered shell of the brave R' Binyamin re-entered the factory. A trail of fresh blood filled the measured footsteps behind him. His body was shattered, but his spirit remained vibrant. He rejoined the friends whose intervention had saved his life.

But R' Binyamin did not arrive alone. Following close behind was the sinister profile of Jonas. A vicious smile was etched on his face. His terror, apparently, was not over.

"This violation will not soon be forgotten," he barked. I will return shortly. And when I do, I expect to see these religious articles ablaze in a fire. If not, all of you will perish." Jonas turned and left the scene, his threat echoing loudly after he was gone.

But these men had already risked their lives for the treasured *tefillin*. One more test would not stop them. They turned to R' Binyamin. Without speaking, he returned to his workbench and picked up a saw and a file. By now he had learned a bit of carpentry. It didn't take long to see that R' Binyamin had begun to fashion small boxes. They were in the shape of *tefillin batim*, boxes. The others pitched in swiftly and in a few minutes a makeshift replica of the holy *tefillin* were formed! Some began to make the fire — Jonas could return any second!

PROFILES and PERSONALITIES מידות

PROFILES AND PERSONALITIES מדות

With the flames shooting skyward and Jonas approaching, they uttered a short prayer and cast the boxes into the fire. And then, brilliantly, they removed the belts from their pants and threw them in too. The black leather straps, hidden amidst the embers, might just look similar enough to the *tefillin retzuos*, straps.

In walked Jonas. Directly to the fire he marched. Peering at the flames, he smiled. "That's better," he offered proudly. "Much better. That could have been all of you." Jonas turned his back to leave, unaware of the tearful group he left behind.

Clutching the holy *tefillin*, R' Binyamin and the others cried and prayed together, in thanks to God. The *tefillin*, like them, had survived. Having something to die for, gave them something to live for.

❦ ❦ ❦

R' Binyamin, and the *tefillin*, went on to survive the torture and horrors of Markstadt and six other concentration camps. And while R' Binyamin passed on just four years ago, the *tefillin* are still very much alive. A *sofer*, scribe, recently affirmed the *tefillin's* validity, but advised against anyone's using the fragile *tefillin* on a regular basis.

But the memories and unforgettable dedication of R' Binyamin will never be forgotten. Each one of his precious grandsons has the privilege of putting on these same *tefillin* when they become *bar mitzvah*. If only a small measure of R' Binyamin's *kedushah*, holiness, is transmitted to them through those *tefillin*, the fire of commitment to *mitzvos* will burn inside them for many generations to come.

told by: Mrs. Rivka Schachner and her children

~§ A Sign of Greatness

In 1954 a young *bochur* still in his teens, left 'the Mesifta' [Torah Vodaas] in Williamsburg where he had been studying, to go to learn in what was then considered one of the most prominent Yeshivos in America, Beis Medrash Elyon in Spring Valley, New York. The Rosh Yeshivah there at the time was one of the *Gedolei HaDor*, Torah Giants of the generation, Rav Reuvain Grozovsky (1896-1958) son-in-law of the world renowned Kamenitzer Rosh Yeshivah, Rav Boruch Ber Leibowitz (1870-1941).

When the *bochur* came to the Yeshiva, Rav Reuvain was already quite ill. He had suffered a stroke which left the right side of his body paralyzed. The *bochurim* who came to learn in Beis Medrash Elyon took turns spending the night in the Rosh Yeshivah's bedroom in case he needed assistance. In the morning, he would wash the Rosh Yeshivah's left (and only mobile) hand and hold a *siddur* for him so he could recite the *Birchas HaShachar*, morning blessings. The *bochur* would respond with *"Amen"* and put the Rosh Yeshivah's *tefillin* on his arm and head.

Assisting Rav Reuvain was not an easy task, for at that point in his life he was confined to bed and he was usually lying on his paralyzed right side. Additionally, his left, mobile hand, would sometimes jerk spontaneously and uncontrollably, making the putting on of his *tefillin* quite difficult.

On this particular *bochur's* first morning assisting Rav Reuvain he was noticeably nervous, for this would be the first time that he would be up close to this world-renowned Rosh Yeshivah he had heard so much about. He had been forewarned that his tasks might not be easy, but he was hoping for the best. What happened was the worst.

As soon as he heard Rav Reuvain stir, the *bochur* came into his room. As he had been instructed by those who had done the job before, he filled a cup of water, held it in one hand and held a large basin in the other hand to catch the water as it poured off Rav Reuvain's hand.

He approached the bed with great trepidation. Rav Reuvain, lying on his side, extended his left hand so that the *bochur,* whom he had never seen before, could pour the water over it. But as the young *bochur* began pouring the water, Rav Reuvain uncontrollably pulled his hand back, causing the water to go straight from the cup into the basin. The *bochur* felt foolish and somewhat helpless but knew he

would have to try again.

He took a step closer to the bed as Rav Reuvain once again extended his thin, wavering hand. The *bochur* poured water but in his haste and nervousness to pour the water before the hand might pull back, he mistakenly poured water onto the bed where it splashed all over the sheet and onto Rav Reuvain's clothes. The young boy was flabbergasted and humiliated to a level he had never experienced before! He wanted to fall into a crevice and hide from humanity. But he still had his chores to complete and then had to go to the morning *minyan* in the *Beis Medrash*.

He tried once again this time with a determined effort not to spill any water except on the Rosh Yeshivah's hands. He finally managed to accomplish it, as he poured the water three times. He wiped Rav Reuvain's hand, and then got a *siddur* from which Rav Reuvain read the *brachos* out loud. As Rav Reuvain peered into the *siddur*, the young *bochur* could not take his eyes off the drenched sheet. He answered *"amen"* dutifully and, still embarrassed, he proceeded to put on the Rosh Yeshivah's *tefillin*.

He turned to leave so that he could get to the *minyan* on time, but then he heard the Rosh Yeshivah call him.

"Yes," he replied.

"What is your name?" Rav Reuvain inquired.

"Yisrael Belsky," the *bochur* answered.

Rav Reuvain asked him to sit down and then he engaged him in some small talk. The Rosh Yeshivah inquired about his family, his former Rosh Yeshivah and about his current *chavrusos*, study partners. Slowly, the *bochur* began to relax as Rav Reuvain thanked him for being of assistance. He told him not to be concerned about what had happened earlier. After a few minutes Rav Reuvain bid the young man good day and wished him *hatzlachah*, success, in his stay at Beis Medrash Elyon.

The *bochur* left the home of Rav Reuvain relaxed. He had undergone a disastrous morning but the calming voice of the Rosh Yeshivah had settled him.

The next day, when the *bochur* retold what had transpired between him and Rav Reuvain, the *bochurim*, students, in the Beis Medrash were shocked! Not one of them could recall Rav Reuvain having ever spoken with his tefillin on! Quickly *bochurim* began asking one another and inquiring from the other Roshei Yeshivah as well, if anyone had ever heard Rav Reuvain talk once he had his *tefillin* on?

It soon became established (and later confirmed by family members) that from the day Rav Reuvain matured, he never intentionally uttered a word (aside from those of prayer and Torah) while wearing his *tefillin*. And yet the day before, for the sake of a *bochur* whom he did not know, who had become so uncomfortable and humiliated in his presence, Rav Reuvain felt compelled to break a precept he had adhered to so fiercely. He spoke freely while donning his *tefillin* only to calm a young *bochur* so that his day of learning and sense of self-worth would not be destroyed.

Now, decades later, Rav Yisrael Belsky, who himself has nurtured thousands of *talmidim*, remembers that incident as the shining example of a Rebbi's sensitivity to a *talmid*, student. Experiencing that event bespoke an eloquence unsurpassed by any lecture.

from the forthcoming book of *"The Maggid"* series by
Rabbi Paysach J. Krohn

PROFILES אישים AND PERSONALITIES מדות

∾§ Checking Plus

The liberation of the Old City of Jerusalem during the 1967 War marked the beginning of a new era for world Jewry. Most prominent among the holy sites that were reclaimed was the *Kosel Ma'aravi*, Western Wall — the last remnant of the Temple Mount structures that surrounded the *Beis Hamikdash*, Holy Temple, prior to its destruction. Now, nearly 25 years later, hundreds of thousands of tears have been shed there in joy, in prayer, and in sorrow.

One of the very first *'simchas'* that took place at the *kosel* was the *bar mitzvah* of Avrohom Yechiel Sukenik, a Queens resident, whose parents utilized the backdrop of the *kosel* to provide an added spark of inspiration and *kedushah* for this landmark event. Friends and relatives journeyed from cities far and wide to participate in this historic occasion — one of the first *bar mitzvahs* at the *kosel*.

The *bar mitzvah* proceedings and celebration were indeed memorable, but the true inspiration — and lesson for life — came after the *tefillin* were folded up and the breakfast tables were cleared.

PROFILES AND PERSONALITIES מידות

Avraham Yechiel, along with his father and uncle, received an invitation from his grandfather, R' Shlomo Zev Sukenik.

"I'm staying at the Kings Hotel," he told them. "Meet me in my room in ten minutes."

When they entered the hotel room, Zeide motioned to Avraham Yechiel to sit beside him. With love and sincerity he spoke to his grandson.

"Today you are *bar mitzvah* and a *bar chiyuvah*, obligated to perform *mitzvos*. And a *mitzvah* that is of supreme importance is that of giving *tzedakah*, charity."

At that point he reached into his drawer and produced a new checkbook with a stack of checks, which prominently displayed the name AVRAHAM YECHIEL SUKENIK.

"In order to properly acquaint you with this most significant *mitzvah*," he continued, "I have opened a checking account in your name and deposited 13,000 *lirah*." (At that time a *lirah* was equivalent to about 30 cents).

Then, Mr. Sukenik handed his sons a long list of worthy Israeli organizations. The next few hours were spent with the sons writing out checks and with Avraham Yechiel affixing his proud, youthful signature to them. They didn't stop until all 13,000 *lirah* were distributed to *tzedakah*.

This incredible experience clearly made an indelible impression on the young lad. Later that evening, Avraham Yechiel was counting the cash that he had received throughout that unforgettable *bar mitzvah* day, from the many guests who participated in the *simchah*. It totalled some 1,800 *lira*. When asked how he planned to spend his newfound treasury he replied, "Well, let's just deposit it into the account and write some more checks!" And so they did.

Several days later, when the family reunited once again in New York, R' Shlomo Zev put the finishing touch on his model lesson.

"The Torah teaches us that no one ever loses money by giving *tzedakah*," he told his grandson. "Somehow the amount distributed — plus more — finds its way back to the original owner." With that introduction he handed Avraham Yechiel an envelope with an additional sum of money.

"Here is my gift for you," he said, "And always remember this great *mitzvah*."

He did.

The Surprise Guest

The Steipler Gaon, Rabbi Yaakov Yisrael Kanievsky, appeared at a *bar mitzvah* celebration in Bnei Brak at precisely the time indicated on the invitation. It was several years since the Steipler had left his house to attend a *simchah* outside of his immediate family. The family of the *bar mitzvah* boy and the handful of early arrivals were astounded to see him. What could have prompted the great *rav* to attend this *simchah*?

The Steipler asked to speak to the *bar mitzvah* boy privately for a few moments. The family was astonished in a different way when the *bar mitzvah* boy explained what had happened. Once, when he was seven years old, he had *davened*, prayed, in the Lederman *shul* in the same *minyan* as the Steipler. The Steipler had noticed a book in the boy's hand and had become annoyed. The book seemed to be a *Gemara*, Talmud, the boy was learning instead of praying. For that, the Steipler gave the child a stern lecture.

Later he discovered, however, that the boy had indeed been praying, but that his *siddur* was laid out in the format of a *Gemara*, with the text in the center of the page, surrounded by commentaries. Pained at having wrongly upset the child, the Steipler asked the boy's name and age. He wanted to ask the boy to forgive him, but since minors do not have the capacity to forgive, he made a mental note that was still sharp six years later. Thus, when the night of the boy's *bar mitzvah* arrived and the child became of age, the Steipler rushed to ask his forgiveness for the unjust reprimand of six years earlier.

The Power of *Tefillin*

A band of thieves once stalked the home of the Vilna Gaon and surmised that great treasures could probably be found there. As the acknowledged leader of the Jewish people of his era, Reb Eliyahu had, undoubtedly, acquired a small fortune which could easily be stolen.

Total fools they were not. Valuable commodities were indeed quite prevalent in the residence of the Vilna Gaon. The precious resources, however, were not of the materialistic variety, but rather of the spiritual

PROFILES and PERSONALITIES מידות

kind. His Torah. His penetrating wisdom. His *ahavas yisrael*, love for his fellow Jew.

The burglars entered through the front of the house where they confronted a room full of erudite scholars who were students of the Vilna Gaon. Inflicting injury and threatening further violence, the perpetrators demanded to know the whereabouts of the treasures in the home.

Meanwhile, in an adjoining room, sat the Vilna Gaon himself, immersed in his learning and in "full uniform" — wearing his *talis* and *tefillin*. Distracted by the noise and commotion from the front of the house, R' Eliyahu interrupted his study and came in to investigate the cause of the disturbance. To his shock, he found himself face to face with the menacing bandits.

Before he could say a word or even shriek for help, the thieves, cowering in sheer terror, made a sudden about-face and fled from the home.

In a mixture of bewilderment and total relief, the disciples crowded around their Rebbe to ask for an explanation. "We have just witnessed a miracle," they said. "Why did the robbers flee as soon as the Rebbe came into the room?"

The *Gaon* immediately pointed to the *tefillin* that were resting on his head. "It is because of the *pasuk*, verse, in *Parshas Ki Savo (Deut. 28:10)*: ,,וְרָאוּ כָּל עַמֵּי הָאָרֶץ כִּי שֵׁם ה' נִקְרָא עָלֶיךָ וְיָרְאוּ מִמֶּךָ'' *"And all the nations of the world will see that the name Hashem is called upon you; and they shall fear you."*

"R' Eliezer Hagadol," continued the *Gra*, "interpreted this verse to refer to the *tefillin shel rosh (Menachos 35b)*. That is why they feared the very sight of me so greatly."

"If so," inquired the students, "why did they not fear us? We, too, were wearing *tefillin*?!"

The *Gaon* responded brilliantly, "Look carefully at the words of R' Eliezer. He did not say the *tefillin shel harosh*, the *tefillin* that are on the head. He said, the *"tefillin sheb' rosh,"* the *tefillin* that are *in* the head! It is not sufficient to simply place the *tefillin* on one's head as an ornament. One must incorporate the holiness and the message of the *tefillin into* one's head — then one truly does one have the name of God upon him."

A PRAYER FOR THE BAR MITZVAH BOY

A Prayer for the Bar Mitzvah Boy
תְּפִלָּה לְיוֹם בַּר־מִצְוָה
מֵאֵת רַבִּי אֱלִיעֶזֶר פַּאפּוֹ בַּעַל פֶּלֶא יוֹעֵץ״ זצ״ל
(the "Pelle Yoetz") zt"l (1785-1828)

רִבּוֹנוֹ שֶׁל עוֹלָם, הֲרֵינִי בָּא לְפָנֶיךָ בְּשִׂמְחָה רַבָּה עַל שֶׁהֶחֱיִיתָנִי וְקִיַּמְתָּנִי וְהִגַּעְתָּנִי לַזְּמַן הַזֶּה. מַה נִּכְבָּד הַיּוֹם הַזֶּה בְּעֵינַי, אֲשֶׁר בּוֹ אֲנִי נִכְנָס בְּגֶדֶר בַּר־מִצְוָה וּמֵעַתָּה אֲנִי מְצֻוֶּה בְּכָל מִצְוֹתֶיךָ, עַל זוֹ שָׂמַח לִבִּי, כִּי הוֹדַעְתָּנוּ עַל־יְדֵי עֲבָדֶיךָ חַכְמֵי יִשְׂרָאֵל, כִּי בְּהַגִּיעַ הָאִישׁ הַיִּשְׂרְאֵלִי אוֹר לְאַרְבָּעָה עָשָׂר שָׁנָה, רוּחַ נָכוֹן יִתְחַדֵּשׁ בְּקִרְבּוֹ, וְגַם אֲשֶׁר נִגְלָה, יֵצֶר־הַטּוֹב הִנֵּה בָא לַעֲזוֹר וּלְהוֹעִיל וְלַעֲשׂוֹת רְצוֹן אָבִינוּ שֶׁבַּשָּׁמַיִם.

עַל הַכֹּל יהוה אֱלֹהֵינוּ אֲנַחְנוּ מוֹדִים לָךְ וּמְהַלְלִים אֶת שְׁמֶךָ, יְהִי שֵׁם יהוה מְבֹרָךְ וּמְרֹמָם עַל כָּל בְּרָכָה וּתְהִלָּה. וְאוּלָם רְעָדָה אֲחָזַתְנִי כִּי יָדַעְתִּי חֶרְפָּתִי בָּשְׁתִּי וּכְלִימָתִי שֶׁעַד עַתָּה הוֹצֵאתִי יָמַי לָרִיק וּשְׁנוֹתַי לַבֶּהָלָה וְקִצַּרְתִּי מְאֹד בַּעֲבוֹדָתֶךָ וְשׁוּם מַעֲשֶׂה טוֹב לֹא עָשִׂיתִי, וְחוֹשְׁשַׁנִי לִי פֶּן חַס וְשָׁלוֹם לֹא אֶהְיֶה כְּלִי מוּכָן וְלֹא אֶזְכֶּה לְרוּחַ נָכוֹן, עַל זֶה הָיָה דָוֶה לִבִּי, וְאַף לָזֹאת יֶחֱרַד לִבִּי כִּי מֵעַתָּה אֲנִי בַּר עוֹנָשִׁין וְחוֹשְׁשַׁנִי לִי פֶּן חַס וְשָׁלוֹם יִתְגַּבֵּר עָלַי יִצְרִי הָרָע וְלֹא אוּכַל לוֹ וְיַעֲבִירֵנִי עַל דַּעַת קוֹנִי, אֵלֶּה אֶזְכְּרָה וְאֶשְׁפְּכָה עָלַי נַפְשִׁי, תְּרוּפָה לֹא מָצָאתִי כִּי אִם לְהַפִּיל תְּחִנָּתִי לְפָנֶיךָ כִּי אַתָּה שׁוֹמֵעַ תְּפִלַּת כָּל פֶּה וְעוֹשֶׂה צְדָקָה עִם כָּל בָּשָׂר וָרוּחַ.

וּבְכֵן שְׁמַע יהוה קוֹלִי אֶקְרָא וְחָנֵּנִי וַעֲנֵנִי, חַטֹּאת נְעוּרַי וּפְשָׁעַי אַל תִּזְכֹּר כְּחַסְדְּךָ זְכָר לִי אַתָּה לְמַעַן טוּבְךָ יהוה לֵב טָהוֹר בְּרָא לִי אֱלֹהִים וְרוּחַ נָכוֹן חַדֵּשׁ בְּקִרְבִּי, הָשִׁיבָה לִי שְׂשׂוֹן יִשְׁעֶךָ וְרוּחַ נְדִיבָה תִסְמְכֵנִי, וְהַשְׁפַּע עָלַי מִמָּרוֹם שֶׁפַע קְדֻשָּׁה וְטַהֲרָה לְעָבְדְּךָ בֶּאֱמֶת תָּמִיד כָּל הַיָּמִים עֲבוֹדָה שְׁלֵמָה עֲבוֹדָה תַמָּה בְּיִרְאָה וְאַהֲבָה וְשִׂמְחָה רַבָּה כְּדַת מַה לַעֲשׂוֹת, וְרִשְׁפֵּי הִתְעוֹרְרוּת אַהֲבָתְךָ וְיִרְאָתְךָ יַתְמִידוּ וְיִתְרַבּוּ בִּי בְּלִי הֶפְסֵק וְתַרְחִיקֵנִי מִיֵּצֶר־הָרָע, וְתַדְבִּיקֵנִי בְּיֵצֶר־הַטּוֹב.

אָנָּא אֶהְיֶה אֲשֶׁר אֶהְיֶה הֱיֵה עוֹזֵר לִי בְּתוֹךְ כֹּל יִשְׂרָאֵל עַמֶּךָ, עָזְרֵנוּ אֱלֹהֵי יִשְׁעֵנוּ עַל דְּבַר כְּבוֹד שְׁמֶךָ וְסַיְּעֵנוּ לְהִתְחַזֵּק בְּתוֹרָתְךָ וְיִרְאָתְךָ וּלְהַתְמִיד בַּעֲבוֹדָתְךָ וְלַעֲשׂוֹת רְצוֹנְךָ כֹּל יְמֵי חַיֵּינוּ, וְלֹא נֶחֱטָא לָךְ וְלֹא לִבְרִיּוֹתֶיךָ וּתְקַנֵּנוּ מַלְכֵּנוּ בְּעֵצָה טוֹבָה מִלְּפָנֶיךָ, וְנִהְיֶה שְׁלֵמִים בְּמִדּוֹת וּבְדֵעוֹת וּבְכָל מִינֵי שְׁלֵמוּת, וְלֹא תֵצֵא מִתַּחַת יָדֵינוּ שׁוּם דָּבָר שֶׁאֵינוּ מְתֻקָּן, וְנִמְצָא חֵן וְשֵׂכֶל טוֹב בְּעֵינֵי אֱלֹהִים וְאָדָם, וְזַכֵּנוּ לְהַשְׁלִים תִּקּוּן נַפְשֵׁנוּ רוּחֵנוּ וְנִשְׁמָתֵנוּ בְּגִלְגּוּל זֶה וְלֹא נֵיעוֹל בְּכִסּוּפָא קַמָּךְ.

A PRAYER
תְּפִלָּה
FOR THE
לְיוֹם
BAR MITZVAH
בַּר מִצְוָה
BOY

אָבִינוּ שֶׁבַּשָּׁמַיִם אַתָּה יוֹדֵעַ אֶת יֵצֶר לֵב הָאָדָם רַע מִנְּעוּרָיו וְהוּא אֵשׁ וַאֲנַחְנוּ בָּשָׂר וָדָם, רְאֵה נָא בְעָנְיֵנוּ וּזְכֹר כִּי עָפָר אֲנַחְנוּ וּרְאֵה כִּי אָזְלַת יָד וְאֶפֶס עָצוּר וְעָזוּב, וּמוֹשִׁיעַ אֵין בִּלְתֶּךָ וְאֵין לָנוּ מֶלֶךְ עוֹזֵר וְסוֹמֵךְ אֶלָּא אָתָּה, עָזְרֵנוּ עַל דְּבַר כְּבוֹד שְׁמֶךָ וַעֲשֵׂה אֲשֶׁר בְּחֻקֶּיךָ נֵלֵךְ וְאָרְחוֹתֶיךָ נִשְׁמֹר וְנַעֲשֶׂה רְצוֹנְךָ כָּל־יְמֵי חַיֵּינוּ, וְנִזְכֶּה וְנִחְיֶה וְנִירַשׁ טוֹבָה וּבְרָכָה לְחַיֵּי הָעוֹלָם הַבָּא לְמַעַן יְזַמֶּרְךָ כָבוֹד וְלֹא יִדֹּם יהוה אֱלֹהַי לְעוֹלָם אוֹדֶךָּ. וּמִבִּרְכָתְךָ יְבֹרַךְ בֵּית עַבְדֶּךָ אָבִי רוֹעִי וְתַאֲרִיךְ יָמָיו בַּטּוֹב וּשְׁנוֹתָיו בַּנְּעִימִים וְלֹא יִגַּע לָרִיק, יִשְׂמַח אָבִי בְּיוֹצְאֵי חֲלָצָיו וְתָגֵל אִמִּי בִּפְרִי בִטְנָהּ בִּרְאוֹתָם אוֹתִי שָׁלֵם בְּמִדּוֹת וּבְדֵעוֹת וּבְכָל־מִינֵי שְׁלֵמוּת. [כשאין לו אב ואם רח״ל, יאמר: וּזְכוּת אָבִי וְאִמִּי עִם זְכוּת כָּל הַצַּדִּיקִים יַעֲמֹד לִי וְהֵם יַמְלִיצוּ בַעֲדִי וִיבַקְשׁוּ רַחֲמִים עָלַי לִפְנֵי כִסֵּא כְבוֹדֶךָ שֶׁתַּעַזְרֵנִי עַל דְּבַר כְּבוֹד שְׁמֶךָ וּתְגַדְּלֵנִי בְּתוֹרָתֶךָ וְיִרְאָתֶךָ וְיִשְׂמַח אָבִי בְּגַן עֵדֶן בְּיוֹצְאֵי חֲלָצָיו וְתָגֵל אִמִּי לְמִצְוֹת בִּפְרִי בִטְנָהּ.]

וּכְשֵׁם שֶׁהֶחֱיִיתַנִי וְהִגַּעְתָּנִי כֵּן תְּחַיֵּינִי וּתְקַיְּמֵנִי וְתַגִּיעֵנִי לְחֻפָּה וּלְמַעֲשִׂים טוֹבִים, וְעַד זִקְנָה וְשֵׂיבָה אֱלֹהִים אַל תַּעַזְבֵנִי, עֲנֵנִי יהוה עֲנֵנִי פְּנֵה אֵלַי וְחָנֵּנִי תְּנָה עֻזְּךָ לְעַבְדֶּךָ וְהוֹשִׁיעָה לְבֶן אֲמָתֶךָ, עֲשֵׂה עִם עַבְדְּךָ כְחַסְדֶּךָ וְחֻקֶּיךָ לַמְּדֵנִי, טוֹב אַתָּה וּמֵטִיב לַמְּדֵנִי חֻקֶּיךָ, הַדְרִיכֵנִי בַּאֲמִתֶּךָ וְלַמְּדֵנִי כִּי אַתָּה אֱלֹהֵי יִשְׁעִי אוֹתְךָ קִוִּיתִי כָּל הַיּוֹם, גַּל עֵינַי וְאַבִּיטָה נִפְלָאוֹת מִתּוֹרָתֶךָ, עֲשֵׂה לְמַעַן רַחֲמֶיךָ הָרַבִּים וּלְמַעַן אֲבוֹתֵינוּ הַקְּדוֹשִׁים אַבְרָהָם יִצְחָק וְיִשְׂרָאֵל עֲבָדֶיךָ. יִהְיוּ לְרָצוֹן אִמְרֵי פִי וְהֶגְיוֹן לִבִּי לְפָנֶיךָ יהוה צוּרִי וְגוֹאֲלִי.

Master of the Universe, I now come before You with great joy since You have sustained me and allowed me to reach this time of life. How glorious is this day in my eyes, as I enter into the category of bar mitzvah, obligated now to perform all of Your commandments. All this gladdens my heart and raises my self-dignity. But I am also delightful to learn through Your servants, the Sages of Israel, that when a Jewish boy reaches the eve of his fourteenth year he is infused with a righteous spirit. It is also accompanied by a yetzer tov, Good Inclination, which assists me in praising Your Name, may it be blessed and exalted beyond all blessings and psalms; all in order to fulfill the wishes of our Father in Heaven — for all this we thank You.

Nevertheless, a great fear has gripped me, for I recognize that I am deeply ashamed and embarrassed for not having spent my years productively. I am, therefore, concerned that, God forbid, I may not be an appropriate receptacle and will prove unworthy to receive Your spirit of righteousness. Because of this I have despaired and trembled. For now I am responsible for my actions and I fear that my yetzer hara, Evil Inclination, will force me to succumb and violate the wishes of my Creator — indeed, this is what I contemplate and my soul is torn asunder.

I have found no remedy but to pour out my supplication before You — for You hear the prayers of all, and render just kindness to all mankind. And so, listen, O God, to my crying voice and answer me. Dismiss the sins and omissions of my youth. Remember me only with kindness, for the sake of Your goodness, O God. Almighty God, create in me a pure heart, and instill a righteous spirit within me.

Restore in me the wellspring of Your salvation and bestow in me a noble spirit. May You infuse in me from above, a holy and pure inclination to always serve You in earnest; each day a complete service — performed with awe, love, and great joy in knowing just what to do. And the inspirational feelings of love and awe for You, should constantly permeate me, without interruption. Distance me from the evil inclination and bind me to the good inclination.

Please, God of Eternity, help me together with Your People, Israel. Assist us, O God of our salvation, for the sake of Your Name's glory and lend aid to fortify us in Your Torah and in Your awe. Help us to be diligent in Your service to fulfill Your will all the days of our lives, so that we will not sin against You or Your creations. Set us upright, our King, with good counsel from before Your Presence, so that we will be complete in character and perspective and in all forms of perfection. Let no harm or improper deed emerge from our hands. May we find favor and understanding in the eyes of God and man, and may we be privileged to perfect our spirit and soul in this lifetime, without shame before You.

Our Father in Heaven, You know that Man's inclination is evil from his youth — that it is a fire and we are mere flesh and blood. Observe us in our distress, for we are dust. And see that without You we are nothing, abandoned — only You are the salvation, for we have no King, help or support but You. Assist us for the sake of Your Name's glory. Help us walk in Your ways and observe Your paths, to fulfill Your will all the days of our lives. May we merit to live and see and inherit goodness and blessing for the life of the World to Come. So that my soul might sing to You and not be stilled, Hashem, my God, forever will I thank You.

And from Your blessings, may the house of my father, my shepherd, be blessed. May his days be extended in goodness and his years in pleasantry. His efforts should not be in vain. His offspring should bring him happiness and my mother should take pleasure in her progeny, when they see my perfection in character and perspective.

A PRAYER תפלה FOR THE ליום BAR MITZVAH בר מצוה BOY

a PRAYER
תפלה
FOR THE
ליום
BAR MITZVAh
בר מצוה
BOY

Just as You have sustained and guided me to this day, so too should You lead me to the wedding canopy and to perform good deeds. And until old age, O Lord, never desert me.

Answer me, God, answer me. Turn to me and show me Your countenance. Give strength to Your servant and save the son of Your hand-maiden. Administer kindness to Your servant and teach me Your statutes. Open my eyes so that I might see the wonders of Your Torah.

Act for the sake of Your mercy and for the sake of our holy forefathers — Abraham, Isaac, and Israel Your servants. And also for the sake of Moses, Aaron, Joseph, and David, and for all the righteous ones, may their merits shield us and may they promote good for us. Act for Your sake, if not for ours.

May the expressions of my mouth and the thoughts of my heart find favor before You, Hashem, my Rock and my Redeemer.

CELEBRATION
and
COMMEMORATION

The Order of Those Called Up to the *Torah*

The Torah reading for the Sabbath of the bar mitzvah is a time when friends and relatives share in the simchah by reciting blessings over the Torah. This important event can be forever recorded, with space designated for each person called up to the Torah, to be filled in before or after the bar mitzvah. There is room for the Kohen, Levite and the Israelites, with room for additional aliyos to be inscribed. The names of a favorite uncle or family friend are eternally inscribed in your book of memories. As in many communities, the maftir blessing is reserved for the bar mitzvah boy on his special day of joy.

ויעזר ויגן ויושיע לכל החוסים בו ונאמר אמן.
הכל הבו גדל לאלהינו ותנו כבוד לתורה.

GUEST LIST

CELEBRATION and COMMEMORATION

Name	Address	Reply Yes	Reply No	Gift	Thank You Sent

GUEST LIST

CELEBRATION and COMMEMORATION

Name	Address	Reply Yes	No	Gift	Thank You Sent

GUEST LIST

CELEBRATION and COMMEMORATION

הלכי מצוה

Name	Address	Reply		Gift	Thank You Sent
		Yes	No		

photographs

photographs

AUTOGRAPHS

AUTOGRAPHS

BAR MITZVAH SPEECH

Rabbi's speech

✑ List of Art Plates

GRACE ברכת AFTER המזון MEALS

The following pages were selected from the popular Manuscript Shiron, Hebrew / English Edition, commissioned by Debbie and Elliot Gibber.

GRACE בִּרְכַּת AFTER הַמָּזוֹן meals

IF I FORGET YOU O JERUSALEM LET MY RIGHT HAND'S SKILL BE FORGOTTEN

PSALM 137 IS SAID ON WEEKDAYS TO REMEMBER THE DESTRUCTION OF THE HOLY TEMPLE.

RETURN THE COHANIM TO THEIR SERVICE AND THE LEVITES TO THEIR SONGS AND HYMNS

PSALM 126 IS SAID ON שַׁבָּת AND יוֹם טוֹב. IT DESCRIBES THE JOY OF THE FUTURE REDEMPTION

RIVERS OF BABYLON. THERE WE SAT AND WE ALSO WEPT WHEN WE REMEMBERED ZION. UPON ITS WILLOWS IN ITS MIDST WE HUNG OUR LYRES. FOR THERE OUR CAPTORS DEMANDED SONG OF US, FROM OUR INSTRUMENTS JOYOUS MELODY. "SING TO US FROM THE SONGS OF ZION!" HOW CAN WE SING THE SONG OF HASHEM ON FOREIGN SOIL? IF I FORGET YOU, O JERUSALEM, LET MY RIGHT HAND'S SKILL BE FORGOTTEN. LET MY TONGUE CLEAVE TO MY PALATE IF I DON'T REMEMBER YOU, IF I FAIL TO ELEVATE JERUSALEM ABOVE MY HIGHEST JOY. REMEMBER HASHEM FOR THE DESCENDANTS OF EDOM, WHO SAY "RAZE IT, RAZE IT TO ITS

OF ASCENTS. WHEN HASHEM WILL RETURN THE CAPTIVES OF ZION WE WILL HAVE BEEN LIKE DREAMERS. THEN OUR MOUTHS WILL BE FILLED WITH LAUGHTER AND OUR TONGUES WITH MIRTH. THEN IT WILL BE SAID AMONG THE NATIONS, "HASHEM HAS DONE GREAT THINGS FOR THEM." HASHEM HAS DONE GREAT THINGS WITH US, AND WE WILL REJOICE. RETURN, HASHEM, OUR CAPTIVES LIKE STREAMS IN THE DESERT. THOSE WHO SOW WITH TEARS WILL REAP IN JUBILATION. HE WALKS ON, WEEPING, CARRYING A LOAD OF SEED, BUT HE WILL RETURN WITH JUBILATION, CARRYING HIS SHEAVES.

VERY FOUNDATION." DAUGHTER OF BABYLON WHO IS LAID TO WASTE, FORTUNATE IS HE WHO REPAYS YOU FOR WHAT YOU HAVE DONE TO HER. FORTUNATE IS HE WHO GRASPS AND SHATTERS YOUR INFANTS AGAINST THE ROCK.

זִמּוּן לִסְעוּדָה

IF THREE OR MORE MALES OVER 13 YEARS OLD ATE TOGETHER, THE LEADER ASKS THEM TO JOIN IN BENCHING

THE LEADER BEGINS:	רַבּוֹתַי נְבָרֵךְ
THE GROUP RESPONDS:	יְהִי שֵׁם יְיָ מְבֹרָךְ מֵעַתָּה וְעַד עוֹלָם.
THE LEADER CONTINUES:	יְהִי שֵׁם יְיָ מְבֹרָךְ מֵעַתָּה וְעַד עוֹלָם.
WHEN TEN MALES OVER 13 YEARS OLD ARE PRESENT, ADD THE WORD IN PARENTHESES:	בִּרְשׁוּת מָרָנָן וְרַבָּנָן וְרַבּוֹתַי נְבָרֵךְ (אֱלֹהֵינוּ) שֶׁאָכַלְנוּ מִשֶּׁלּוֹ.
THE GROUP RESPONDS:	בָּרוּךְ (אֱלֹהֵינוּ) שֶׁאָכַלְנוּ מִשֶּׁלּוֹ וּבְטוּבוֹ חָיִינוּ.
THE LEADER CONTINUES:	בָּרוּךְ (אֱלֹהֵינוּ) שֶׁאָכַלְנוּ מִשֶּׁלּוֹ וּבְטוּבוֹ חָיִינוּ.
ALL RESPOND QUIETLY:	בָּרוּךְ הוּא וּבָרוּךְ שְׁמוֹ.

GRACE
ברכת
AFTER
המזון
MEALS

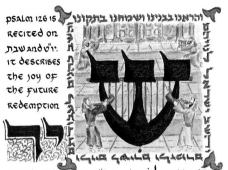

PSALM 126 15 RECITED ON שבת AND יו"ט IT DESCRIBES THE JOY OF THE FUTURE REDEMPTION

PSALM 137 15 RECITED ON WEEKDAYS TO REMEMBER THE TEMPLE'S DESTRUCTION

נְהָרוֹת בָּבֶל שָׁם יָשַׁבְנוּ הַמַּעֲלוֹת בְּשׁוּב יְיָ אֶת
גַּם בָּכִינוּ בְּזָכְרֵנוּ אֶת צִיוֹן: שִׁיבַת צִיוֹן הָיִינוּ כְּחֹלְמִים: אָז
עַל עֲרָבִים בְּתוֹכָהּ תָּלִינוּ יִמָּלֵא שְׂחוֹק פִּינוּ וּלְשׁוֹנֵנוּ
כִּנֹּרוֹתֵינוּ: כִּי שָׁם שְׁאֵלוּנוּ רִנָּה: אָז יֹאמְרוּ בַגּוֹיִם
שׁוֹבֵינוּ דִּבְרֵי שִׁיר וְתוֹלָלֵנוּ הִגְדִּיל יְיָ לַעֲשׂוֹת עִם אֵלֶּה:
שִׂמְחָה שִׁירוּ לָנוּ מִשִּׁיר הִגְדִּיל יְיָ לַעֲשׂוֹת עִמָּנוּ הָיִינוּ
צִיּוֹן: אֵיךְ נָשִׁיר אֶת שִׁיר שְׂמֵחִים: שׁוּבָה יְיָ אֶת שְׁבִיתֵנוּ
יְיָ עַל אַדְמַת נֵכָר: אִם כַּאֲפִיקִים בַּנֶּגֶב: הַזֹּרְעִים
אֶשְׁכָּחֵךְ יְרוּשָׁלָיִם תִּשְׁכַּח בְּדִמְעָה בְּרִנָּה יִקְצֹרוּ: הָלוֹךְ יֵלֵךְ
יְמִינִי: תִּדְבַּק לְשׁוֹנִי לְחִכִּי וּבָכֹה נֹשֵׂא מֶשֶׁךְ הַזָּרַע בֹּא
אִם לֹא אֶזְכְּרֵכִי אִם לֹא יָבֹא בְרִנָּה נֹשֵׂא אֲלֻמֹּתָיו:
אַעֲלֶה אֶת יְרוּשָׁלַיִם עַל רֹאשׁ

שִׂמְחָתִי: זְכֹר יְיָ לִבְנֵי אֱדוֹם אֵת יוֹם יְרוּשָׁלָיִם הָאֹמְרִים עָרוּ
עָרוּ עַד הַיְסוֹד בָּהּ: בַּת בָּבֶל הַשְּׁדוּדָה אַשְׁרֵי שֶׁיְשַׁלֶּם לָךְ אֶת
גְּמוּלֵךְ שֶׁגָּמַלְתְּ לָנוּ: אַשְׁרֵי שֶׁיֹּאחֵז וְנִפֵּץ אֶת עֹלָלַיִךְ אֶל הַסָּלַע:

זִמּוּן לִסְעוּדָה

IF THREE OR MORE MALES OVER 13 YEARS OLD ATE TOGETHER, THE LEADER ASKS THEM TO JOIN IN BENCHING

THE LEADER BEGINS: רַבּוֹתַי נְבָרֵךְ.
THE GROUP RESPONDS: יְהִי שֵׁם יְיָ מְבֹרָךְ מֵעַתָּה וְעַד עוֹלָם.
THE LEADER CONTINUES: יְהִי שֵׁם יְיָ מְבֹרָךְ מֵעַתָּה וְעַד עוֹלָם.
WHEN TEN MALES OVER 13 YEARS OLD ARE PRESENT, ADD THE WORD IN PARENTHESES: בִּרְשׁוּת מָרָנָן וְרַבָּנָן וְרַבּוֹתַי נְבָרֵךְ (אֱלֹהֵינוּ) שֶׁאָכַלְנוּ מִשֶּׁלּוֹ.
THE GROUP RESPONDS: בָּרוּךְ (אֱלֹהֵינוּ) שֶׁאָכַלְנוּ מִשֶּׁלּוֹ וּבְטוּבוֹ חָיִינוּ.
THE LEADER CONTINUES: בָּרוּךְ (אֱלֹהֵינוּ) שֶׁאָכַלְנוּ מִשֶּׁלּוֹ וּבְטוּבוֹ חָיִינוּ.
ALL RESPOND QUIETLY: בָּרוּךְ הוּא וּבָרוּךְ שְׁמוֹ.

GRACE
ברכת
AFTER
המזון
meals

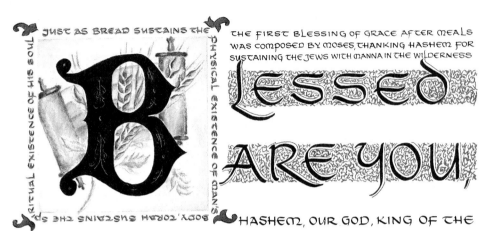

JUST AS BREAD SUSTAINS THE

THE FIRST BLESSING OF GRACE AFTER MEALS
WAS COMPOSED BY MOSES, THANKING HASHEM FOR
SUSTAINING THE JEWS WITH MANNA IN THE WILDERNESS

lessed
ARE YOU,

HASHEM, OUR GOD, KING OF THE
UNIVERSE, WHO NOURISHES THE ENTIRE WORLD WITH HIS
GOODNESS, WITH FAVOR, LOVINGKINDNESS AND WITH MERCY.
HE GIVES NOURISHMENT TO ALL FLESH, BECAUSE HIS LOVING-
KINDNESS IS ETERNAL, AND THROUGH HIS ABUNDANT GOODNESS
WE HAVE NEVER BEEN LACKING AND MAY WE NEVER BE LACKING
FOREVER AND EVER. FOR THE SAKE OF HIS GREAT NAME,
BECAUSE HE IS ALMIGHTY AND PROVIDES FOOD FOR ALL,
AND HE BENEFITS ALL AND PROVIDES FOR THE NEEDS OF
ALL OF HIS CREATURES WHICH HE HAS CREATED. BLESSED
ARE YOU, HASHEM, WHO SUSTAINS ALL.

THE SECOND BLESSING WAS COMPOSED BY JOSHUA IN
THANKS TO HASHEM FOR GIVING US THE LAND OF ISRAEL

WE GIVE THANKS TO YOU, HASHEM, OUR GOD, THAT
YOU HAVE BEQUEATHED TO OUR FOREFATHERS A DESIRABLE,
GOOD AND SPACIOUS LAND; AND BECAUSE YOU HAVE BROUGHT
US OUT, HASHEM, OUR GOD, FROM THE LAND OF EGYPT, AND
REDEEMED US FROM THE HOUSE OF BONDAGE; AND FOR
YOUR COVENANT WHICH YOU HAVE SEALED IN OUR FLESH
AND FOR YOUR TORAH WHICH YOU HAVE TAUGHT US, AND
FOR YOUR STATUTES WHICH YOU HAVE MADE KNOWN TO
US; AND FOR THE LIFE, GRACE AND LOVINGKINDNESS WITH
WHICH YOU HAVE FAVORED US; AND FOR THE FOOD WHICH
WE HAVE EATEN THROUGH WHICH YOU NOURISH AND MAINTAIN
US CONSTANTLY, EVERY DAY, IN EVERY SEASON, AND AT
ANY HOUR.

GRACE
בְּרְכַת
AFTER
הַמָּזוֹן
meals

THE FIRST BLESSING OF בִּרְכַּת הַמָּזוֹן WAS COMPOSED BY MOSES. IT THANKS GOD FOR GIVING THE JEWS MANNA TO SUSTAIN THEM WHILE IN THE WILDERNESS.

בָּרוּךְ אַתָּה יְיָ אֱלֹהֵינוּ

מֶלֶךְ הָעוֹלָם הַזָּן אֶת
הָעוֹלָם כֻּלּוֹ בְּטוּבוֹ בְּחֵן בְּחֶסֶד וּבְרַחֲמִים
הוּא נֹתֵן לֶחֶם לְכָל בָּשָׂר כִּי לְעוֹלָם חַסְדּוֹ.
וּבְטוּבוֹ הַגָּדוֹל תָּמִיד לֹא חָסַר לָנוּ וְאַל
יֶחְסַר לָנוּ מָזוֹן לְעוֹלָם וָעֶד. בַּעֲבוּר שְׁמוֹ
הַגָּדוֹל כִּי הוּא אֵל זָן וּמְפַרְנֵס לַכֹּל וּמֵטִיב
לַכֹּל וּמֵכִין מָזוֹן לְכָל בְּרִיּוֹתָיו אֲשֶׁר בָּרָא.
בָּרוּךְ אַתָּה יְיָ הַזָּן אֶת הַכֹּל:

THE SECOND BLESSING WAS COMPOSED BY JOSHUA
IN THANKS TO GOD FOR GIVING US THE LAND OF ISRAEL

יְיָ אֱלֹהֵינוּ עַל שֶׁהִנְחַלְתָּ
לַאֲבוֹתֵינוּ אֶרֶץ חֶמְדָּה
טוֹבָה וּרְחָבָה. וְעַל שֶׁהוֹצֵאתָנוּ יְיָ אֱלֹהֵינוּ
מֵאֶרֶץ מִצְרַיִם וּפְדִיתָנוּ מִבֵּית עֲבָדִים וְעַל
בְּרִיתְךָ שֶׁחָתַמְתָּ בִּבְשָׂרֵנוּ וְעַל תּוֹרָתְךָ שֶׁלִּמַּדְתָּנוּ
וְעַל חֻקֶּיךָ שֶׁהוֹדַעְתָּנוּ וְעַל חַיִּים חֵן וָחֶסֶד
שֶׁחוֹנַנְתָּנוּ וְעַל אֲכִילַת מָזוֹן שָׁאַתָּה זָן וּמְפַרְנֵס
אוֹתָנוּ תָּמִיד בְּכָל יוֹם וּבְכָל עֵת וּבְכָל שָׁעָה:

GRACE ברכת AFTER המזון meals

ON CHANUKAH חנוכה על, A PRAYER OF THANKSGIVING IS ADDED, COMMEMORATING THE MIRACULOUS VICTORY OF THE JEWS OVER ANTIOCHUS AND THE SYRIAN-GREEKS.

FOR THE MIRACLES AND FOR THE REDEMPTION, AND FOR THE MIGHTY DEEDS, AND FOR THE DELIVERANCES, AND FOR THE WARS THAT YOU PERFORMED FOR OUR FOREFATHERS IN THOSE DAYS AT THIS TIME:

IN THE DAYS OF MATISYAHU, SON OF YOCHANON, THE HIGH PRIEST, THE HASHMONEAN AND HIS SONS, WHEN THE EVIL GREEK EMPIRE ROSE UP AGAINST YOUR NATION, ISRAEL, TO MAKE THEM FORGET YOUR TORAH, AND TO TURN THEM FROM THE STATUTES OF YOUR WILL. AND YOU, IN YOUR GREAT MERCY, STOOD UP FOR THEM IN THEIR TIME OF DISTRESS. YOU FOUGHT THEIR STRUGGLE, JUDGED THEIR JUDGMENT, AVENGED THEIR WRONG. YOU DELIVERED THE STRONG INTO THE HANDS OF THE WEAK, THE MANY INTO THE HANDS OF THE FEW, THE WICKED INTO THE HANDS OF THE RIGHTEOUS, THE DEFIANT SINNERS INTO THE HANDS OF THOSE WHO STUDY YOUR TORAH. AND FOR YOURSELF YOU MADE A GREAT AND HOLY NAME, AND FOR YOUR NATION ISRAEL, YOU'VE WROUGHT GREAT SALVATION AND REDEMPTION AS THIS VERY DAY. AND THEN YOUR CHILDREN CAME INTO YOUR HOLY OF HOLIES, AND CLEANSED YOUR TEMPLE, PURIFIED YOUR SANCTUARY, KINDLED LIGHTS IN YOUR HOLY COURTYARDS, AND DESIGNATED THESE EIGHT DAYS OF CHANUKAH, TO GIVE THANKS AND PRAISE TO YOUR HOLY NAME.

GRACE בְּרְכַּת
AFTER הַמָּזוֹן
MEALS

on chanukah הַנִּסִּים עַל, a prayer of thanksgiving is added, commemorating the miraculous victory of the jews over antiochus and the syrian-greeks

עַל הַנִּסִּים וְעַל הַפֻּרְקָן וְעַל הַגְּבוּרוֹת וְעַל הַתְּשׁוּעוֹת וְעַל הַמִּלְחָמוֹת שֶׁעָשִׂיתָ לַאֲבוֹתֵינוּ בַּיָּמִים הָהֵם בַּזְּמַן הַזֶּה:

בִּימֵי מַתִּתְיָהוּ בֶּן יוֹחָנָן כֹּהֵן גָּדוֹל חַשְׁמוֹנָאִי וּבָנָיו כְּשֶׁעָמְדָה מַלְכוּת יָוָן הָרְשָׁעָה עַל עַמְּךָ יִשְׂרָאֵל לְהַשְׁכִּיחָם תּוֹרָתֶךָ וּלְהַעֲבִירָם מֵחֻקֵּי רְצוֹנֶךָ. וְאַתָּה בְּרַחֲמֶיךָ הָרַבִּים עָמַדְתָּ לָהֶם בְּעֵת צָרָתָם, רַבְתָּ אֶת רִיבָם, דַּנְתָּ אֶת דִּינָם נָקַמְתָּ אֶת נִקְמָתָם. מָסַרְתָּ גִבּוֹרִים בְּיַד חַלָּשִׁים, וְרַבִּים בְּיַד מְעַטִּים, וּטְמֵאִים

בְּיַד טְהוֹרִים, וּרְשָׁעִים בְּיַד צַדִּיקִים, וְזֵדִים בְּיַד עוֹסְקֵי תוֹרָתֶךָ. וּלְךָ עָשִׂיתָ שֵׁם גָּדוֹל וְקָדוֹשׁ בְּעוֹלָמֶךָ וּלְעַמְּךָ יִשְׂרָאֵל עָשִׂיתָ תְּשׁוּעָה גְדוֹלָה וּפֻרְקָן כְּהַיּוֹם הַזֶּה. וְאַחַר כַּךְ בָּאוּ בָנֶיךָ לִדְבִיר בֵּיתֶךָ וּפִנּוּ אֶת הֵיכָלֶךָ וְטִהֲרוּ אֶת מִקְדָּשֶׁךָ וְהִדְלִיקוּ נֵרוֹת בְּחַצְרוֹת קָדְשֶׁךָ וְקָבְעוּ שְׁמוֹנַת יְמֵי חֲנֻכָּה אֵלּוּ לְהוֹדוֹת וּלְהַלֵּל לְשִׁמְךָ הַגָּדוֹל:

Grace After Meals ☐ 171

GRACE בְּרָכָּה AFTER הַמָּזוֹן meals

ON PURIM עַל הַנִּסִּים, A PRAYER OF THANKSGIVING IS RECITED. IT COMMEMORATES ESTHER AND MORDECHAI'S ROLE IN HELPING SAVE THE JEWS FROM HAMAN'S PLOT.

FOR THE MIRACLES AND FOR THE REDEMPTION, AND FOR THE MIGHTY DEEDS, AND FOR THE DELIVERANCES, AND FOR THE WARS THAT YOU PERFORMED FOR OUR FOREFATHERS IN THOSE DAYS AT THIS TIME:

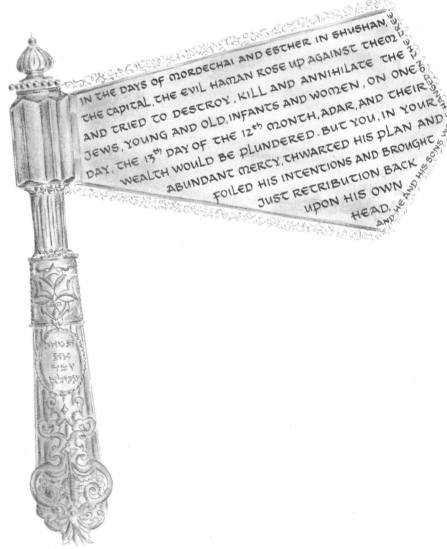

IN THE DAYS OF MORDECHAI AND ESTHER IN SHUSHAN, THE CAPITAL, THE EVIL HAMAN ROSE UP AGAINST THEM AND TRIED TO DESTROY, KILL AND ANNIHILATE THE JEWS, YOUNG AND OLD, INFANTS AND WOMEN, ON ONE DAY, THE 13th DAY OF THE 12th MONTH, ADAR, AND THEIR WEALTH WOULD BE PLUNDERED. BUT YOU, IN YOUR ABUNDANT MERCY, THWARTED HIS PLAN AND FOILED HIS INTENTIONS AND BROUGHT JUST RETRIBUTION BACK UPON HIS OWN HEAD. AND HE AND HIS SONS WERE HANGED ON THE...

GRACE בּרכת AFTER המזון meals

On purim על הנסים, a prayer of thanksgiving, is recited. It commemorates esther and mordechai's role in helping save the jews from haman's plot.

עַל הַנִּסִּים וְעַל הַפֻּרְקָן
וְעַל הַגְּבוּרוֹת
וְעַל הַתְּשׁוּעוֹת וְעַל הַמִּלְחָמוֹת שֶׁעָשִׂיתָ
לַאֲבוֹתֵינוּ בַּיָּמִים הָהֵם בַּזְּמַן הַזֶּה:

בִּימֵי מָרְדְּכַי וְאֶסְתֵּר בְּשׁוּשַׁן הַבִּירָה כְּשֶׁעָמַד עֲלֵיהֶם הָמָן הָרָשָׁע בִּקֵּשׁ לְהַשְׁמִיד לַהֲרֹג וּלְאַבֵּד אֶת כָּל הַיְּהוּדִים מִנַּעַר וְעַד זָקֵן טַף וְנָשִׁים בְּיוֹם אֶחָד בִּשְׁלוֹשָׁה עָשָׂר לְחֹדֶשׁ שְׁנֵים עָשָׂר הוּא חֹדֶשׁ אֲדָר וּשְׁלָלָם לָבוֹז וְאַתָּה בְּרַחֲמֶיךָ הָרַבִּים הֵפַרְתָּ אֶת עֲצָתוֹ וְקִלְקַלְתָּ אֶת מַחֲשַׁבְתּוֹ וַהֲשֵׁבוֹתָ לוֹ גְּמוּלוֹ בְּרֹאשׁוֹ וְתָלוּ אוֹתוֹ וְאֶת בָּנָיו עַל הָעֵץ.

GRACE
ברכת
AFTER
המזון
MEALS

AND FOR ALL THINGS, HASHEM, OUR GOD, WE THANK AND BLESS YOU. MAY YOUR NAME BE BLESSED IN THE MOUTH OF ALL LIVING THINGS, ALWAYS AND FOREVER, AS IT IS WRITTEN,"AND YOU SHALL EAT AND BE SATISFIED, AND YOU SHALL BLESS HASHEM YOUR GOD FOR THE GOOD LAND WHICH HE HAS GIVEN TO YOU." BLESSED ARE YOU, HASHEM, FOR THE LAND AND FOR THE FOOD.

RETURN TO YOUR CITY JERUSALEM, WITH COMPASSION … AND REBUILD IT SOON, IN OUR DAYS, AS AN ETERNAL BUILDING

THE THIRD BLESSING WAS COMPOSED BY KING DAVID AS A PRAYER FOR JERUSALEM, WITH A PRAYER FOR THE בית המקדש LATER ADDED BY KING SOLOMON

LEASE, HASHEM, OUR GOD, HAVE COMPASSION ON ISRAEL, YOUR NATION AND ON JERUSALEM, YOUR HOLY CITY AND ON ZION THE SANCTUARY OF YOUR GLORY, AND ON THE KINGSHIP OF DAVID, YOUR ANNOINTED AND ON THE GREAT AND HOLY HOUSE UPON WHICH YOUR NAME IS CALLED. OUR GOD, OUR FATHER , TEND US, NOURISH US, SUSTAIN AND MAINTAIN US, RELIEVE US AND GRANT US RELIEF, HASHEM, OUR GOD, SPEEDILY FROM ALL OUR DISTRESS, AND PLEASE, HASHEM, OUR GOD , DO NOT MAKE US DEPENDENT UPON GIFTS FROM THE HANDS OF MAN , AND NOT UPON THEIR LOANS, BUT ONLY UPON YOUR FULL, OPEN, HOLY AND BOUNTIFUL HAND, THAT WE MAY NEVER BE EMBARASSED OR ASHAMED.

GRACE ברכת AFTER המזון meals

on shabbos add the following:

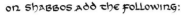

רְצֵה וְהַחֲלִיצֵנוּ

יְיָ אֱלֹהֵינוּ בְּמִצְוֹתֶיךָ וּבְמִצְוַת יוֹם הַשְּׁבִיעִי הַשַּׁבָּת הַגָּדוֹל וְהַקָּדוֹשׁ הַזֶּה כִּי יוֹם זֶה גָּדוֹל וְקָדוֹשׁ הוּא לְפָנֶיךָ לִשְׁבָּת בּוֹ וְלָנוּחַ בּוֹ בְּאַהֲבָה כְּמִצְוַת רְצוֹנֶךָ וּבִרְצוֹנְךָ הָנִיחַ לָנוּ יְיָ אֱלֹהֵינוּ שֶׁלֹּא תְהֵא צָרָה וְיָגוֹן וַאֲנָחָה בְּיוֹם מְנוּחָתֵנוּ וְהַרְאֵנוּ יְיָ אֱלֹהֵינוּ בְּנֶחָמַת צִיּוֹן עִירֶךָ וּבְבִנְיַן יְרוּשָׁלַיִם עִיר קָדְשֶׁךָ כִּי אַתָּה הוּא בַּעַל הַיְשׁוּעוֹת וּבַעַל הַנֶּחָמוֹת:

on rosh chodesh and festivals add the following,
inserting the appropriate phrase

אֱלֹהֵינוּ וֵאלֹהֵי אֲבוֹתֵינוּ

יַעֲלֶה וְיָבֹא

וְיַגִּיעַ וְיֵרָאֶה וְיֵרָצֶה וְיִשָּׁמַע וְיִפָּקֵד וְיִזָּכֵר זִכְרוֹנֵנוּ וּפִקְדוֹנֵנוּ וְזִכְרוֹן אֲבוֹתֵינוּ וְזִכְרוֹן מָשִׁיחַ בֶּן דָּוִד עַבְדֶּךָ וְזִכְרוֹן יְרוּשָׁלַיִם עִיר קָדְשֶׁךָ וְזִכְרוֹן כָּל עַמְּךָ בֵּית יִשְׂרָאֵל לְפָנֶיךָ לִפְלֵיטָה לְטוֹבָה לְחֵן וּלְחֶסֶד וּלְרַחֲמִים לְחַיִּים וּלְשָׁלוֹם בְּיוֹם

shavuos	passover	rosh chodesh
חַג הַשָּׁבֻעוֹת	חַג הַמַּצּוֹת	רֹאשׁ הַחֹדֶשׁ

shmini atzeres/simchas torah	succos	rosh hashanah
הַשְּׁמִינִי חַג הָעֲצֶרֶת	חַג הַסֻּכּוֹת	הַזִּכָּרוֹן

הַזֶּה . זָכְרֵנוּ יְיָ אֱלֹהֵינוּ בּוֹ לְטוֹבָה . וּפָקְדֵנוּ בוֹ לִבְרָכָה . וְהוֹשִׁיעֵנוּ בוֹ לְחַיִּים טוֹבִים . וּבִדְבַר יְשׁוּעָה וְרַחֲמִים חוּס וְחָנֵּנוּ וְרַחֵם עָלֵינוּ וְהוֹשִׁיעֵנוּ כִּי אֵלֶיךָ עֵינֵינוּ כִּי אֵל מֶלֶךְ חַנּוּן וְרַחוּם אָתָּה:

Grace After Meals □ 177

GRACE AFTER MEALS

ברכת המזון

REBUILD JERUSALEM

THE HOLY CITY, SPEEDILY IN OUR DAYS. BLESSED ARE YOU, HASHEM, WHO REBUILDS JERUSALEM IN HIS COMPASSION, AMEN.

BLESSED ARE YOU, HASHEM, OUR GOD, KING OF THE UNIVERSE, THE ALMIGHTY, OUR FATHER, OUR KING, OUR MIGHTY ONE, OUR CREATOR, OUR REDEEMER, OUR MAKER, OUR HOLY ONE, THE HOLY ONE OF JACOB, OUR SHEPHERD, THE SHEPHERD OF ISRAEL, THE GOOD KING WHO BESTOWS GOODNESS TO ALL, FOR ON EVERY SINGLE DAY, HE DID GOOD, HE DOES GOOD AND WILL DO GOOD FOR US, HE HAS BENEFITED US HE BENEFITS US, AND WILL BENEFIT US FOREVER WITH FAVOR, WITH LOVINGKINDNESS, AND WITH COMPASSION, AND WITH RELIEF, RESCUE AND SUCCESS, BLESSING AND SALVATION, COMFORT, SUSTENANCE AND SUPPORT AND COMPASSION, LIFE AND PEACE AND ALL GOODNESS, FROM ALL GOODNESS MAY HE NEVER DEPRIVE US.

THE COMPASSIONATE ONE MAY HE RULE OVER US FOREVER AND EVER.
THE COMPASSIONATE ONE MAY HE BE BLESSED IN THE HEAVENS AND ON EARTH.
THE COMPASSIONATE ONE MAY HE BE PRAISED FOR ALL GENERATIONS, AND MAY HE BE GLORIFIED THROUGH US FOR ALL THE EVERLASTING ETERNITIES, AND MAY HE BE HONORED THROUGH US ETERNALLY.

ברכת
AFTER
המזון
meals

וּבְנֵה יְרוּשָׁלַיִם

עִיר הַקֹּדֶשׁ בִּמְהֵרָה בְיָמֵינוּ.

בָּרוּךְ אַתָּה יְיָ בּוֹנֵה בְרַחֲמָיו יְרוּשָׁלָיִם. אָמֵן:

בָּרוּךְ אַתָּה יְיָ
אֱלֹהֵינוּ

THE FOURTH BLESSING WAS COMPOSED BY RABBAN GAMLIEL'S
COURT IN THANKS TO GOD FOR PRESERVING THE BODIES OF
BETAR'S VICTIMS AND ALLOWING THEM TO BE PROPERLY BURIED

מֶלֶךְ הָעוֹלָם הָאֵל אָבִינוּ מַלְכֵּנוּ אַדִירֵנוּ בּוֹרְאֵנוּ
גּוֹאֲלֵנוּ יוֹצְרֵנוּ קְדוֹשֵׁנוּ קְדוֹשׁ יַעֲקֹב רוֹעֵנוּ רוֹעֵה
יִשְׂרָאֵל הַמֶּלֶךְ הַטּוֹב וְהַמֵּטִיב לַכֹּל שֶׁבְּכָל יוֹם
וָיוֹם הוּא הֵטִיב הוּא מֵטִיב הוּא יֵיטִיב לָנוּ.
הוּא גְמָלָנוּ הוּא גוֹמְלֵנוּ הוּא יִגְמְלֵנוּ לָעַד לְחֵן
וּלְחֶסֶד וּלְרַחֲמִים וּלְרֶוַח הַצָּלָה וְהַצְלָחָה
בְּרָכָה וִישׁוּעָה נֶחָמָה פַּרְנָסָה וְכַלְכָּלָה
וְרַחֲמִים וְחַיִּים וְשָׁלוֹם וְכָל טוֹב וּמִכָּל טוּב
לְעוֹלָם אַל יְחַסְּרֵנוּ:

הָרַחֲמָן הוּא יִמְלוֹךְ עָלֵינוּ לְעוֹלָם וָעֶד.
הָרַחֲמָן הוּא יִתְבָּרַךְ בַּשָּׁמַיִם וּבָאָרֶץ.
הָרַחֲמָן הוּא יִשְׁתַּבַּח לְדוֹר דּוֹרִים וְיִתְפָּאַר
בָּנוּ לָעַד וּלְנֶצַח נְצָחִים וְיִתְהַדַּר
בָּנוּ לָעַד וּלְעוֹלְמֵי עוֹלָמִים.

GRACE בִּרְכַּת AFTER הַמָּזוֹן MEALS

THE COMPASSIONATE ONE, MAY HE SUSTAIN US HONORABLY.

THE COMPASSIONATE ONE, MAY HE BREAK THE YOKE FROM OUR NECKS, AND MAY HE LEAD US UPRIGHT TO OUR LAND.

THE COMPASSIONATE ONE, MAY HE SEND US A BOUNTIFUL BLESSING IN THIS HOUSE AND ON THIS TABLE FROM WHICH WE HAVE EATEN.

THE COMPASSIONATE ONE, MAY HE SEND US ELIJAH THE PROPHET, HIS MEMORY BE BLESSED, THAT HE MAY ANNOUNCE TO US GOOD TIDINGS, SALVATIONS AND COMFORTS.

THIS BLESSING, FOUND IN THE TALMUD (BERACHOS 46A) IS RECITED BY A GUEST FOR HIS HOST
MAY IT BE YOUR WILL THAT THE HOST OF THIS HOUSE NOT BE SHAMED OR EMBARASSED, NOT IN THIS WORLD NOR IN THE WORLD TO COME. MAY HE BE SUCCESSFUL IN ALL HIS ENDEAVORS, AND MAY HIS ENDEAVORS BE SUCCESSFUL AND CLOSE TO THE CITY, AND MAY NO EVIL RULE OVER THE WORK OF HIS HAND, AND MAY NO OBJECT OF SIN OR THOUGHT OF INIQUITY BE FOUND BEFORE HIM NOW AND FOREVER.

THE COMPASSIONATE ONE, MAY HE BLESS (MY FATHER, MY TEACHER) THE HOST OF THIS HOUSE AND (MY MOTHER, MY TEACHER) THE HOSTESS OF THIS HOUSE, THEM AND THEIR CHILDREN AND ALL THAT IS THEIRS.

GUESTS ADD THE PHRASES SHOWN: CHILDREN AT THEIR PARENTS' TABLE ADD THE WORDS IN PARENTHESES

THOSE EATING AT THEIR OWN TABLE ADD THE WORDS IN PARENTHESES AS THEY APPLY
ME (AND MY WIFE / MY HUSBAND / MY CHILDREN) AND ALL THAT IS MINE

ALL CONTINUE HERE

US AND ALL THAT IS OURS, JUST AS OUR FOREFATHERS, ABRAHAM, ISAAC AND JACOB WERE BLESSED IN ALL THINGS, FROM EVERYTHING, WITH EVERYTHING, SO SHALL HE BLESS ALL OF US TOGETHER, WITH A COMPLETE BLESSING AND LET US SAY, AMEN.

IN THE CELESTIAL HEIGHTS, MAY THERE BE A MERIT PLEADED FOR THEM AND FOR US, THAT IT SHOULD BE A PROTECTION OF PEACE, AND MAY WE RECEIVE A BLESSING FROM HASHEM AND RIGHTEOUSNESS FROM OUR GOD OF SALVATION AND MAY WE FIND FAVOR AND BENEFICIAL UNDERSTANDING IN THE EYES OF GOD AND MAN.

הָרַחֲמָן הוּא יְפַרְנְסֵנוּ בְּכָבוֹד.

הָרַחֲמָן הוּא יִשְׁבֹּר עֻלֵּנוּ מֵעַל צַוָּארֵנוּ וְהוּא יוֹלִיכֵנוּ קוֹמְמִיּוּת לְאַרְצֵנוּ.

הָרַחֲמָן הוּא יִשְׁלַח לָנוּ בְּרָכָה מְרֻבָּה בַּבַּיִת הַזֶּה וְעַל שֻׁלְחָן זֶה שֶׁאָכַלְנוּ עָלָיו.

הָרַחֲמָן הוּא יִשְׁלַח לָנוּ אֶת אֵלִיָּהוּ הַנָּבִיא זָכוּר לַטּוֹב וִיבַשֶּׂר לָנוּ בְּשׂוֹרוֹת טוֹבוֹת יְשׁוּעוֹת וְנֶחָמוֹת.

This blessing, found in the Talmud (Berachos 46a), is recited by a guest for his host.

יְהִי רָצוֹן שֶׁלֹּא יֵבוֹשׁ וְלֹא יִכָּלֵם בַּעַל הַבַּיִת הַזֶּה, לֹא בָעוֹלָם הַזֶּה וְלֹא בָעוֹלָם הַבָּא, וְיַצְלִיחַ בְּכָל נְכָסָיו, וְיִהְיוּ נְכָסָיו מֻצְלָחִים וּקְרוֹבִים לָעִיר, וְאַל יִשְׁלֹט שָׂטָן בְּמַעֲשֵׂה יָדָיו, וְאַל יִזְדַּקֵּק לְפָנָיו שׁוּם דְּבַר חֵטְא וְהִרְהוּר עָוֹן, מֵעַתָּה וְעַד עוֹלָם.

Guests add the following phrases, and children at their parents' table add the words in parentheses.

הָרַחֲמָן הוּא יְבָרֵךְ

אֶת (אָבִי מוֹרִי) בַּעַל הַבַּיִת הַזֶּה וְאֶת (אִמִּי מוֹרָתִי) בַּעֲלַת הַבַּיִת הַזֶּה, אוֹתָם וְאֶת בֵּיתָם וְאֶת זַרְעָם וְאֶת כָּל אֲשֶׁר לָהֶם

Those eating at their own table add the following words in parentheses as they apply

אוֹתִי (וְאֶת אִשְׁתִּי / בַּעְלִי / וְאֶת זַרְעִי) וְאֶת כָּל אֲשֶׁר לִי

all continue here

אוֹתָנוּ וְאֶת כָּל אֲשֶׁר לָנוּ כְּמוֹ שֶׁנִּתְבָּרְכוּ אֲבוֹתֵינוּ אַבְרָהָם יִצְחָק וְיַעֲקֹב בַּכֹּל מִכֹּל כֹּל כֵּן יְבָרֵךְ אוֹתָנוּ כֻּלָּנוּ יַחַד בִּבְרָכָה שְׁלֵמָה וְנֹאמַר אָמֵן:

בַּמָּרוֹם יְלַמְּדוּ עֲלֵיהֶם וְעָלֵינוּ זְכוּת שֶׁתְּהֵא לְמִשְׁמֶרֶת שָׁלוֹם. וְנִשָּׂא בְרָכָה מֵאֵת יְיָ וּצְדָקָה מֵאֱלֹהֵי יִשְׁעֵנוּ וְנִמְצָא חֵן וְשֵׂכֶל טוֹב בְּעֵינֵי אֱלֹהִים וְאָדָם:

GRACE ברכת AFTER המזון MEALS

ON SHABBOS: THE COMPASSIONATE ONE, MAY HE LET US INHERIT A DAY THAT IS ALL SHABBOS AND REST FOR ETERNAL LIFE.

ON ROSH CHODESH: THE COMPASSIONATE ONE, MAY HE RENEW FOR US THIS NEW MONTH FOR GOODNESS AND BLESSING.

ON FESTIVALS: THE COMPASSIONATE ONE, MAY HE LET US INHERIT A DAY THAT IS ALL GOODNESS.

ON ROSH HASHANAH: THE COMPASSIONATE ONE, MAY HE RENEW THE NEW YEAR UPON US FOR GOODNESS AND BLESSING.

ON SUCCOS: THE COMPASSIONATE ONE, MAY HE ERECT FOR US THE FALLEN TABERNACLE OF DAVID.

IF על הנסים WAS NOT RECITED IN ITS PROPER PLACE, RECITE THE FOLLOWING PHRASE AND CONTINUE WITH בימי מתתיהו (ON CHANUKAH, PAGE 10) OR בימי מרדכי (ON PURIM, PAGE 12)

THE COMPASSIONATE ONE, MAY HE PERFORM MIRACLES AND WONDERS FOR US AS HE DID FOR OUR FOREFATHERS IN THOSE DAYS AT THIS TIME.

THE COMPASSIONATE ONE, MAY HE LET US MERIT THE DAYS OF MOSHIACH AND LIFE IN THE WORLD TO COME (ON WEEKDAYS: HE MAKES GREAT SALVATIONS FOR HIS KING) (ON SHABBOS, NEW MOON, FESTIVALS: HE IS A TOWER OF DELIVERANCE FOR HIS KING) AND DOES KINDNESS TO DAVID, HIS ANNOINTED, AND HIS DESCENDANTS FOREVER. HE WHO MAKES PEACE IN HIS CELESTIAL HEIGHTS MAY HE MAKE PEACE FOR US AND FOR ALL ISRAEL, AND SAY, AMEN.

REVERE HASHEM, HIS HOLY ONES, FOR THERE IS NEVER DEPRIVATION FOR THOSE WHO REVERE HIM. YOUNG LIONS MAY BE HUNGRY AND NEEDY, BUT THOSE WHO SEEK HASHEM SHALL NEVER BE DEPRIVED OF ANY GOODNESS. GIVE THANKS TO HASHEM FOR HE IS GOOD, FOR HIS LOVINGKINDNESS IS EVERLASTING. OPEN YOUR HAND, HASHEM, AND SATIATE THE NEEDS OF ALL LIVING THINGS. BLESSED IS THE MAN WHO TRUSTS IN GOD, AND GOD WILL BE HIS SECURITY. I ONCE WAS YOUTHFUL AND I HAVE ALSO AGED, AND I HAVE NEVER SEEN A RIGHTEOUS PERSON FORSAKEN, THAT HIS CHILDREN MUST SEEK BREAD. GOD WILL GIVE MIGHT TO HIS NATION, GOD WILL BLESS HIS NATION WITH PEACE.

on shabbos add:

הָרַחֲמָן הוּא יַנְחִילֵנוּ יוֹם שֶׁכֻּלוֹ שַׁבָּת וּמְנוּחָה לְחַיֵּי הָעוֹלָמִים:

on rosh chodesh add:

הָרַחֲמָן הוּא יְחַדֵּשׁ עָלֵינוּ אֶת הַחֹדֶשׁ הַזֶּה לְטוֹבָה וְלִבְרָכָה:

on festivals add:

הָרַחֲמָן הוּא יַנְחִילֵנוּ יוֹם שֶׁכֻּלוֹ טוֹב:

on rosh hashanah add:

הָרַחֲמָן הוּא יְחַדֵּשׁ עָלֵינוּ אֶת הַשָּׁנָה הַזֹּאת לְטוֹבָה וְלִבְרָכָה:

on succos add:

הָרַחֲמָן הוּא יָקִים לָנוּ אֶת סֻכַּת דָּוִד הַנּוֹפָלֶת:

If עַל הַנִּסִּים was not said in its proper place, recite the following phrase on בִּימֵי מָרְדְּכַי chanukah or on בִּימֵי מַתִּתְיָהוּ purim (pages 6 and 7) and continue with

הָרַחֲמָן הוּא יַעֲשֶׂה לָנוּ נִסִּים וְנִפְלָאוֹת כַּאֲשֶׁר עָשָׂה לַאֲבוֹתֵינוּ בַּיָּמִים הָהֵם בַּזְּמַן הַזֶּה:

הָרַחֲמָן הוּא יְזַכֵּנוּ לִימוֹת הַמָּשִׁיחַ וּלְחַיֵּי הָעוֹלָם הַבָּא. (on weekdays: מַגְדִּל)

(מִגְדּוֹל on shabbos, festivals and rosh chodesh) יְשׁוּעוֹת מַלְכּוֹ וְעֹשֶׂה חֶסֶד לִמְשִׁיחוֹ לְדָוִד וּלְזַרְעוֹ עַד עוֹלָם. עֹשֶׂה שָׁלוֹם בִּמְרוֹמָיו הוּא יַעֲשֶׂה שָׁלוֹם עָלֵינוּ וְעַל כָּל יִשְׂרָאֵל. וְאִמְרוּ אָמֵן:

יְראוּ אֶת יְיָ קְדֹשָׁיו כִּי אֵין מַחְסוֹר לִירֵאָיו. כְּפִירִים רָשׁוּ וְרָעֵבוּ וְדֹרְשֵׁי יְיָ לֹא יַחְסְרוּ כָל טוֹב. הוֹדוּ לַיְיָ כִּי טוֹב כִּי לְעוֹלָם חַסְדּוֹ. פּוֹתֵחַ אֶת יָדֶךָ וּמַשְׂבִּיעַ לְכָל חַי רָצוֹן. בָּרוּךְ הַגֶּבֶר אֲשֶׁר יִבְטַח בַּיְיָ וְהָיָה יְיָ מִבְטַחוֹ. נַעַר הָיִיתִי גַּם זָקַנְתִּי וְלֹא רָאִיתִי צַדִּיק נֶעֱזָב וְזַרְעוֹ מְבַקֶּשׁ לָחֶם. יְיָ עֹז לְעַמּוֹ יִתֵּן יְיָ יְבָרֵךְ אֶת עַמּוֹ בַשָּׁלוֹם.

CONCLUDING על BLESSING המחיה

WHEAT

BARLEY

GRAPES

FIGS

POMEGRANATES

OLIVES

DATES

AFTER EATING FOODS FROM THE FIVE GRAIN SPECIES (WHEAT, OATS, SPELT, BARLEY, RYE) OR WINE, GRAPES, FIGS, OLIVES, DATES, OR POMEGRANATES SAY THE FOLLOWING

BLESSED ARE YOU,

HASHEM, OUR GOD, KING OF THE UNIVERSE, FOR THE

GRAIN PRODUCTS	WINE/GRAPE JUICE	FRUITS (AS ABOVE)
NOURISHMENT AND SUSTENANCE	VINE AND FRUIT OF THE VINE	TREE AND FRUIT OF THE TREE

AND FOR THE PRODUCE OF THE FIELD AND FOR THE LAND WHICH IS DESIRABLE, GOOD AND SPACIOUS THAT YOU WERE PLEASED TO BEQUEATH TO OUR FOREFATHERS, TO EAT FROM ITS FRUITS AND BE SATISFIED FROM ITS GOODNESS. PLEASE HAVE MERCY, HASHEM, OUR GOD, ON ISRAEL, YOUR NATION, AND ON JERUSALEM, YOUR CITY, AND ON ZION, THE DWELLING PLACE OF YOUR GLORY, AND ON YOUR ALTAR AND UPON YOUR TEMPLE. AND REBUILD JERUSALEM, THE HOLY CITY, SPEEDILY, IN OUR DAYS, AND BRING US UP TO ITS MIDST, AND LET US REJOICE IN ITS REBUILDING AND LET US EAT FROM ITS FRUIT, AND BE SATISFIED FROM ITS GOODNESS AND WE WILL BLESS YOU UPON IT IN HOLINESS AND IN PURITY.

ON SHABBOS:	ON ROSH CHODESH:	ON ROSH HASHANAH:
AND BE PLEASED AND LET US REST ON THIS SHABBOS DAY	AND REMEMBER US FOR GOODNESS ON THIS NEW MOON	AND REMEMBER US FOR GOODNESS ON THIS NEW YEAR

ON FESTIVALS ADD: AND GLADDEN US

ON THIS FESTIVAL OF MATZOS	ON THIS FESTIVAL OF SHAVUOS	ON THIS FESTIVAL OF SUCCOS	ON THIS EIGHTH DAY FESTIVAL

FOR YOU, HASHEM, ARE GOOD AND DO GOOD TO ALL AND WE THANK YOU FOR THE LAND AND FOR THE

GRAIN PRODUCTS	WINE/GRAPE JUICE	FRUITS (AS ABOVE)
NOURISHMENT.	FRUIT OF THE VINE.	*FRUITS.

BLESSED ARE YOU, HASHEM, FOR THE LAND AND FOR THE

NOURISHMENT:	FRUIT OF THE VINE:	*FRUITS:

*FOR FRUITS FROM THE LAND OF ISRAEL, SUBSTITUTE 'ITS FRUIT.'

CONCLUDING BLESSING עַל הַמִּחְיָה

AFTER EATING FOODS FROM THE FIVE SPECIES
OF GRAINS, OR WINE, GRAPES, FIGS, OLIVES,
DATES OR POMEGRANATES, SAY THE FOLLOWING:

THE FIVE GRAINS ARE WHEAT, OATS,
SPELT, BARLEY AND RYE

בָּרוּךְ אַתָּה יְיָ אֱלֹהֵינוּ מֶלֶךְ הָעוֹלָם עַל

AFTER FRUITS (FROM THE ABOVE)	AFTER WINE OR GRAPE JUICE	AFTER GRAIN PRODUCTS
הָעֵץ וְעַל פְּרִי הָעֵץ	הַגֶּפֶן וְעַל פְּרִי הַגֶּפֶן	הַמִּחְיָה וְעַל הַכַּלְכָּלָה

וְעַל תְּנוּבַת הַשָּׂדֶה, וְעַל אֶרֶץ חֶמְדָּה טוֹבָה וּרְחָבָה,
שֶׁרָצִיתָ וְהִנְחַלְתָּ לַאֲבוֹתֵינוּ, לֶאֱכוֹל מִפִּרְיָהּ וְלִשְׂבּוֹעַ
מִטּוּבָהּ. רַחֵם (נָא) יְיָ אֱלֹהֵינוּ עַל יִשְׂרָאֵל עַמֶּךָ, וְעַל
יְרוּשָׁלַיִם עִירֶךָ, וְעַל צִיּוֹן מִשְׁכַּן כְּבוֹדֶךָ, וְעַל מִזְבְּחֶךָ
וְעַל הֵיכָלֶךָ. וּבְנֵה יְרוּשָׁלַיִם עִיר הַקֹּדֶשׁ בִּמְהֵרָה
בְיָמֵינוּ, וְהַעֲלֵנוּ לְתוֹכָהּ, וְשַׂמְּחֵנוּ בְּבִנְיָנָהּ, וְנֹאכַל מִפִּרְיָהּ,
וְנִשְׂבַּע מִטּוּבָהּ, וּנְבָרֶכְךָ עָלֶיהָ בִּקְדֻשָׁה וּבְטָהֳרָה.

on ROSH HASHANAH add:	on ROSH CHODESH add:	on SHABBOS add:
וּזְכְרֵנוּ לְטוֹבָה בְּיוֹם הַזִּכָּרוֹן הַזֶּה:	וְזָכְרֵנוּ (לְטוֹבָה) בְּיוֹם רֹאשׁ הַחֹדֶשׁ הַזֶּה:	רְצֵה וְהַחֲלִיצֵנוּ בְּיוֹם הַשַּׁבָּת הַזֶּה:

on FESTIVALS add:

וְשַׂמְּחֵנוּ בְּיוֹם

חַג הַמַּצוֹת הַזֶּה:	חַג הַשָּׁבוּעוֹת הַזֶּה:	חַג הַסֻּכּוֹת הַזֶּה:	הַשְּׁמִינִי חַג הָעֲצֶרֶת הַזֶּה:

כִּי אַתָּה יְיָ טוֹב וּמֵטִיב לַכֹּל, וְנוֹדֶה לְּךָ עַל הָאָרֶץ

וְעַל הַמִּחְיָה.	וְעַל פְּרִי הַגֶּפֶן.	וְעַל הַפֵּרוֹת.

בָּרוּךְ אַתָּה יְיָ עַל הָאָרֶץ

וְעַל הַמִּחְיָה:	וְעַל פְּרִי הַגָּפֶן:	וְעַל הַפֵּרוֹת:

kiddush
קידוש

RECITE QUIETLY:
(AND IT WAS EVENING AND IT WAS MORNING)

THE SIXTH DAY

AND THE HEAVENS AND THE EARTH WERE COMPLETED AND ALL OF THEIR HOSTS. AND GOD COMPLETED ON THE SEVENTH DAY, HIS WORK WHICH HE HAD DONE. AND HE RESTED ON THE SEVENTH DAY FROM ALL HIS WORK WHICH HE HAD DONE. AND GOD BLESSED THE SEVENTH DAY AND SANCTIFIED IT, FOR ON IT HE RESTED FROM ALL HIS WORK WHICH GOD HAD CREATED TO DO.

ATTENTION, OUR MASTERS AND OUR TEACHERS:

BLESSED ARE YOU, HASHEM, OUR GOD, KING OF THE UNIVERSE, WHO CREATES THE FRUIT OF THE VINE: BLESSED ARE YOU, HASHEM, OUR GOD, KING OF THE UNIVERSE, WHO HAS SANCTIFIED US WITH HIS COMMANDMENTS AND WAS PLEASED WITH US, AND HIS HOLY SHABBOS, WITH LOVE AND WITH PLEASURE HE BEQUEATHED TO US, A REMEMBRANCE OF CREATION. FOR THIS DAY IS THE FIRST OF THE HOLY CONVOCATIONS, A MEMORIAL TO OUR EXODUS FROM EGYPT. FOR YOU CHOSE US AND SANCTIFIED US FROM ALL THE NATIONS, AND YOUR HOLY SHABBOS WITH LOVE AND PLEASURE YOU BEQUEATHED TO US. BLESSED ARE YOU, HASHEM, WHO **SANCTIFIES THE SHABBOS:**

(text curving around cup:) WHOEVER MAKES KIDDUSH ON WINE ON FRIDAY NIGHT... HIS DAYS ARE LENGTHENED IN THIS WORLD AND YEARS OF... HE ARE ADDED TO HIM IN THE WORLD TO COME

Kiddush קִידּוּשׁ

(בלחש) וַיְהִי עֶרֶב וַיְהִי בֹקֶר:

יוֹם הַשִּׁשִּׁי

וַיְכֻלּוּ הַשָּׁמַיִם וְהָאָרֶץ
וְכָל צְבָאָם: וַיְכַל אֱלֹהִים
בַּיּוֹם הַשְּׁבִיעִי מְלַאכְתּוֹ
אֲשֶׁר עָשָׂה. וַיִּשְׁבֹּת
בַּיּוֹם הַשְּׁבִיעִי מִכָּל
מְלַאכְתּוֹ אֲשֶׁר עָשָׂה:
וַיְבָרֶךְ אֱלֹהִים אֶת יוֹם הַשְּׁבִיעִי וַיְקַדֵּשׁ
אֹתוֹ כִּי בוֹ שָׁבַת מִכָּל מְלַאכְתּוֹ אֲשֶׁר
בָּרָא אֱלֹהִים לַעֲשׂוֹת:

סַבְרִי מָרָנָן וְרַבָּנָן וְרַבּוֹתַי.

בָּרוּךְ אַתָּה יְיָ אֱלֹהֵינוּ מֶלֶךְ הָעוֹלָם
בּוֹרֵא פְּרִי הַגָּפֶן:

בָּרוּךְ אַתָּה יְיָ אֱלֹהֵינוּ מֶלֶךְ הָעוֹלָם
אֲשֶׁר קִדְּשָׁנוּ בְּמִצְוֹתָיו וְרָצָה בָנוּ
וְשַׁבַּת קָדְשׁוֹ בְּאַהֲבָה וּבְרָצוֹן הִנְחִילָנוּ
זִכָּרוֹן לְמַעֲשֵׂה בְרֵאשִׁית. (כִּי הוּא יוֹם)
תְּחִלָּה לְמִקְרָאֵי קֹדֶשׁ זֵכֶר לִיצִיאַת
מִצְרָיִם. (כִּי בָנוּ בָחַרְתָּ וְאוֹתָנוּ קִדַּשְׁתָּ
מִכָּל הָעַמִּים) וְשַׁבַּת קָדְשְׁךָ בְּאַהֲבָה
וּבְרָצוֹן הִנְחַלְתָּנוּ: בָּרוּךְ אַתָּה יְיָ
מְקַדֵּשׁ הַשַּׁבָּת:

Friday Night Kiddush ☐ 187

Kiddush
קידוש

IF YOU RESTRAIN

BECAUSE OF SHABBOS, YOUR FEET, REFRAIN FROM DOING YOUR PERSONAL DESIRES ON MY HOLY DAY; IF YOU CALL SHABBOS 'A DELIGHT', THE HOLY ONE OF HASHEM, 'AN HONORED ONE,' AND YOU HONOR IT BY NOT DOING YOUR OWN WAYS, FROM SEEKING YOUR PERSONAL DESIRES AND BY NOT DISCUSSING FORBIDDEN MATTERS, THEN SHALL YOU REVEL IN PLEASURE WITH HASHEM, AND I SHALL MOUNT YOU UPON THE HEIGHTS OF THE LAND, AND I SHALL ALLOW YOU TO PARTAKE OF THE LEGACY GIVEN TO JACOB, YOUR FATHER, FOR THE MOUTH OF HASHEM HAS SPOKEN.

AND THE CHILDREN OF ISRAEL GUARDED THE SHABBOS, TO MAKE THE SHABBOS FOR THEIR GENERATIONS AS AN ETERNAL COVENANT. BETWEEN ME AND THE CHILDREN OF ISRAEL, IT IS A SIGN FOREVER, THAT IN SIX DAYS HASHEM MADE THE HEAVENS AND EARTH, AND ON THE SEVENTH DAY CEASED TO CREATE AND HE RESTED

HASHEM SAYS TO YISROEL: MY SONS, BESTOW ON ME HONOR, ACCOUNT AND MAKE KIDDUSH ON THE DAY AND HAVE FAITH IN ME THAT I SHALL REPAY YOU FOR ALL YOU HAVE SPENT IN MY HONOR.

REMEMBER THE DAY OF SHABBOS TO SANCTIFY IT. FOR SIX DAYS YOU WILL LABOR AND DO ALL OF YOUR OWN WORK, BUT ON THE SEVENTH DAY IT IS SHABBOS TO HASHEM YOUR GOD, YOU MAY DO NO WORK, YOU, YOUR SON, YOUR DAUGHTER, YOUR SLAVE AND YOUR MAIDSERVANT, YOUR ANIMALS AND THE STRANGER WHO IS IN YOUR GATES. BECAUSE IN SIX DAYS HASHEM MADE THE HEAVENS AND THE EARTH, THE SEA AND ALL THAT IS IN THEM, AND HE RESTED ON THE SEVENTH DAY.

THEREFORE, HASHEM BLESSED THE SHABBOS DAY, AND MADE IT HOLY:

BLESSED ARE YOU, HASHEM, OUR GOD, KING OF THE UNIVERSE, WHO CREATES THE FRUIT OF THE VINE:

kiddush
קידוש

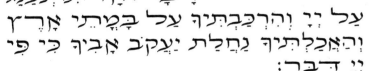

אם תָּשִׁיב מִשַּׁבָּת רַגְלֶךָ עֲשׂוֹת חֲפָצֶךָ בְּיוֹם קָדְשִׁי וְקָרָאתָ לַשַּׁבָּת עֹנֶג לִקְדוֹשׁ יְיָ מְכֻבָּד וְכִבַּדְתּוֹ מֵעֲשׂוֹת דְּרָכֶיךָ מִמְּצוֹא חֶפְצְךָ וְדַבֵּר דָּבָר: אָז תִּתְעַנַּג עַל יְיָ וְהִרְכַּבְתִּיךָ עַל בָּמֳתֵי אָרֶץ וְהַאֲכַלְתִּיךָ נַחֲלַת יַעֲקֹב אָבִיךָ כִּי פִּי יְיָ דִּבֵּר:

וְשָׁמְרוּ בְנֵי יִשְׂרָאֵל אֶת הַשַּׁבָּת לַעֲשׂוֹת אֶת הַשַּׁבָּת לְדֹרֹתָם בְּרִית עוֹלָם: בֵּינִי וּבֵין בְּנֵי יִשְׂרָאֵל אוֹת הִוא לְעוֹלָם כִּי שֵׁשֶׁת יָמִים עָשָׂה יְיָ אֶת הַשָּׁמַיִם וְאֶת הָאָרֶץ וּבַיּוֹם הַשְּׁבִיעִי שָׁבַת וַיִּנָּפַשׁ:

זָכוֹר אֶת יוֹם הַשַּׁבָּת לְקַדְּשׁוֹ: שֵׁשֶׁת יָמִים תַּעֲבֹד וְעָשִׂיתָ כָּל מְלַאכְתֶּךָ: וְיוֹם הַשְּׁבִיעִי שַׁבָּת לַיְיָ אֱלֹהֶיךָ לֹא תַעֲשֶׂה כָל מְלָאכָה אַתָּה וּבִנְךָ וּבִתֶּךָ עַבְדְּךָ וַאֲמָתְךָ וּבְהֶמְתֶּךָ וְגֵרְךָ אֲשֶׁר בִּשְׁעָרֶיךָ: כִּי שֵׁשֶׁת יָמִים עָשָׂה יְיָ אֶת הַשָּׁמַיִם וְאֶת הָאָרֶץ אֶת הַיָּם וְאֶת כָּל אֲשֶׁר בָּם וַיָּנַח בַּיּוֹם הַשְּׁבִיעִי עַל כֵּן בֵּרַךְ יְיָ אֶת יוֹם הַשַּׁבָּת וַיְקַדְּשֵׁהוּ:

סַבְרִי מָרָנָן וְרַבָּנָן וְרַבּוֹתַי

בָּרוּךְ אַתָּה יְיָ אֱלֹהֵינוּ מֶלֶךְ הָעוֹלָם בּוֹרֵא פְּרִי הַגָּפֶן:

havdalah
הבדלה

BEHOLD! GOD OF MY SALVATION. I SHALL TRUST AND WILL NOT FEAR. FOR GOD IS MY MIGHT AND PRAISE, HASHEM, AND HE WAS A SALVATION FOR ME. DRAW WATER WITH JOY FROM THE SPRINGS OF SALVATION. SALVATION IS HASHEM'S, UPON YOUR NATION, YOUR BLESSINGS REST, SELAH. GOD, LORD OF HOSTS IS WITH US, A STRONGHOLD FOR US IN THE GOD OF JACOB, SELAH. GOD, LORD OF HOSTS, PRAISED IS THE MAN WHO TRUSTS IN YOU. HASHEM, SAVE! THE KING WILL RESPOND TO US ON THE DAY THAT WE CALL. FOR THE JEWS THERE WAS LIGHT, GLADNESS, JOY AND HONOR, SO SHALL IT BE FOR US. I LIFT UP A CUP OF SALVATION AND I CALL IN THE NAME OF GOD. **BLESSED** ARE YOU, HASHEM, OUR GOD, KING OF THE UNIVERSE, WHO CREATES THE FRUIT OF THE VINE: **BLESSED** ARE YOU, HASHEM, OUR GOD, KING OF THE UNIVERSE, WHO CREATES THE VARIED SPECIES OF SPICES: **BLESSED** ARE YOU, HASHEM, OUR GOD, KING OF THE UNIVERSE, WHO CREATES THE LIGHT OF FIRE **BLESSED** ARE YOU, HASHEM, OUR GOD, KING OF THE UNIVERSE, WHO DIVIDES BETWEEN HOLY AND SECULAR, BETWEEN LIGHT AND DARKNESS, BETWEEN ISRAEL AND THE NATIONS, BETWEEN THE SEVENTH DAY AND THE SIX DAYS OF LABOR. BLESSED ARE YOU, HASHEM, WHO DIVIDES BETWEEN HOLY AND SECULAR.

havdalah
הבדלה

הבדלה is the distinction between the holy and profane. It is made on wine, on spices, to revive us after losing our נשמה יתרה, and on a candle (of two wicks) as Adam discovered fire on מוצאי שבת.

יְשׁוּעָתִי אֶבְטַח וְלֹא אֶפְחָד,
כִּי עָזִּי וְזִמְרָת יָהּ יְיָ וַיְהִי
לִי לִישׁוּעָה: וּשְׁאַבְתֶּם מַיִם בְּשָׂשׂוֹן, מִמַּעַיְנֵי הַיְשׁוּעָה:
לַיָי הַיְשׁוּעָה, עַל עַמְּךָ בִרְכָתֶךָ סֶּלָה: יְיָ צְבָאוֹת עִמָּנוּ,
מִשְׂגָּב לָנוּ אֱלֹהֵי יַעֲקֹב סֶלָה: יְיָ צְבָאוֹת אַשְׁרֵי אָדָם בֹּטֵחַ
בָּךְ: יְיָ הוֹשִׁיעָה הַמֶּלֶךְ יַעֲנֵנוּ בְיוֹם קָרְאֵנוּ: לַיְּהוּדִים
הָיְתָה אוֹרָה וְשִׂמְחָה וְשָׂשׂוֹן וִיקָר. כֵּן תִּהְיֶה לָּנוּ: כּוֹס
יְשׁוּעוֹת אֶשָּׂא, וּבְשֵׁם יְיָ אֶקְרָא:

בָּרוּךְ אַתָּה יְיָ אֱלֹהֵינוּ מֶלֶךְ הָעוֹלָם
בּוֹרֵא פְּרִי הַגָּפֶן:

בָּרוּךְ אַתָּה יְיָ אֱלֹהֵינוּ מֶלֶךְ הָעוֹלָם
בּוֹרֵא מִינֵי בְשָׂמִים:

בָּרוּךְ אַתָּה יְיָ אֱלֹהֵינוּ מֶלֶךְ הָעוֹלָם
בּוֹרֵא מְאוֹרֵי הָאֵשׁ:

בָּרוּךְ אַתָּה יְיָ אֱלֹהֵינוּ מֶלֶךְ הָעוֹלָם
הַמַּבְדִּיל בֵּין קֹדֶשׁ לְחוֹל בֵּין אוֹר לְחֹשֶׁךְ
בֵּין יִשְׂרָאֵל לָעַמִּים, בֵּין יוֹם הַשְּׁבִיעִי לְשֵׁשֶׁת יְמֵי
הַמַּעֲשֶׂה. בָּרוּךְ אַתָּה יְיָ הַמַּבְדִּיל בֵּין קֹדֶשׁ לְחוֹל:

page

**List of
Artplates**

Bircas

Hamazon
———
**Grace After
Meals**

167. עַל נַהֲרוֹת בָּבֶל — The letter ע, whose name is the Hebrew word for eye, sheds tears as it remembers the beauty of Jerusalem. Nebuchadnezzar asked the Levites to play musical instruments for him, as they did in the Temple. They responded, "Is it not enough that we have caused the destruction of the Temple, do we also have to play for this dwarf (Nebuchadnezzar) and his gods?" (Yalkut Tehillim).

167. שִׁיר הַמַּעֲלוֹת — The Levites played their instruments on the fifteen steps, the מַעֲלוֹת, the steps of the Holy Temple. We ask God to show us the rebuilt Temple, the return of the Kohanim to their service, the Levites to their songs and hymns, and the Israelites to their dwelling places (Festival Liturgy).

169. הַזָּן אֶת הַכֹּל — The Midrash to the Sidrah Noach comments: Said the dove before God, "Master of the Universe, let my sustenance be as bitter as the olive and given by Your hand, and not sweet as honey, but dependent on mortal men."

171. עַל הַנִּסִּים — The stately Chanukah menorah is flanked by the prayer that thanks God for His miracles.

173. עַל הַנִּסִּים — An ornate Megillas Esther contains within it the Al Hanisim prayer, thanking God for Mordechai and Esther's victory over Haman.

175. רַחֵם נָא — The prayer of וְלִירוּשָׁלַיִם עִירְךָ from the weekday liturgy asks God to return to the city of Jerusalem with mercy and to reestablish the kingdom of the House of David.

177. רְצֵה — The Sabbath is the focal point of the creation, as Mechilta explains (Yisro): "In six days God created the heavens and the earth, and rested on the seventh." This teaches that the Sabbath is as important as the other six days of creation combined.

177. יַעֲלֶה וְיָבֹא — God declares to his people: "If you gladden those who depend on Me (i.e. the orphaned, the widowed, etc.) and those who depend on you (i.e. your family and servants) in your house on the festivals, I, too, will gladden those who are Mine and those who are yours in My home, the Holy Temple" (Tanchuma, Re'ei).

179. וּבְנֵה יְרוּשָׁלַיִם — "The rebuilt city of Jerusalem, a city which is connected together" (Psalms 122:3). The Talmud Yerushalmi, Chagigah chap. 6 explains that Jerusalem is the city that unites all Jews as friends.

185. בְּרָכָה אַחַת מֵעֵין שָׁלֹשׁ — God has taken us to a land which is blessed with plenty, therefore the fruits with which Israel is praised require a special after-blessing.

187. יוֹם הַשִּׁשִּׁי — The sixth day. This implies that there is a specific sixth day — the sixth of Sivan on which we received the Torah (Shabbos 88a).

189. קִידוּשׁ הַיּוֹם — Remember the Sabbath to sanctify it (Exodus 20:8). One who mentions the King must bless Him; one who mentions the Sabbath must sanctify it (Zohar, Yisro).

191. הַבְדָּלָה — Three kinds of people merit the World to Come: One who lives in the land of Israel, one who raises his children to study Torah, and one who makes havdalah on wine upon the conclusion of the Sabbath (Pesachim 113a).

192 □ BAR MITZVAH